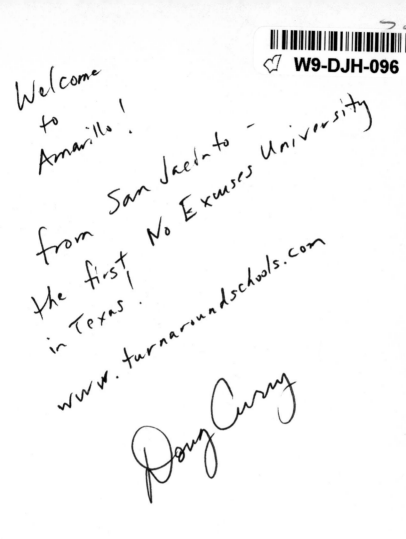

Welcome
to
Amarillo!

from San Jacinto —
the first No Excuses University
in Texas.

www.turnaroundschools.com

Doug Curry

NO EXCUSES
UNIVERSITY™

DAMEN LOPEZ

HUNDREDS OF SCHOOLS • THOUSANDS OF STUDENTS
ONE BIG DREAM

TURNAROUND SCHOOLS PUBLICATIONS

NO EXCUSES UNIVERSITY™

DAMEN LOPEZ

HUNDREDS OF SCHOOLS • THOUSANDS OF STUDENTS
ONE BIG DREAM

ISBN: 978-0-9842154-0-9

LCCN: 2009938081

Available through
www.TurnAroundSchools.com

Printed in China
Printed on recycled paper

DEDICATION

*This book is dedicated to the six women
whose support has made all the
difference in my life.*

*To my wife, Lara,
it is my greatest joy to know that everything
that is written in this book
was first heard by your ears.*

*To my four daughters,
Sophia, Olivia, Mia, and Ava,
who remind me daily that my greatest
accolade is that of being your daddy.*

*And to my mother, Barbara,
who started the entire journey with
a pat on my chest, a kiss
on my forehead, and five little
words whispered at bedtime:
"After high school comes college."*

I love you all very much.

About this Book

As someone who has never forgotten the challenges that teachers face on a daily basis, I want educators to find the words within these pages not only enjoyable to read, but practical as well. I, like many of you, have attended conferences, examined articles, and read books anticipating solutions to everyday challenges that I faced as a teacher and principal. Too many times, however, I was left asking, "What now?" I found few offerings of how I might actually improve my pedagogy. From the moment I began writing this book, I knew that I wanted it to be done so in a format as practitioner-friendly as could be. Because of this, I focused on three strategies as I wrote.

First, I was diligent in writing in a style that might mirror a conversation between two caring professionals. Second, I began each chapter with a Key Concepts section in an effort to frontload the reader. Finally, no chapter was complete until I added a Theory to Practice section at the end. What begins with questions that teams can discuss, ends with step-by-step suggestions that schools can act upon. The Theory to Practice section acts not as a book study, but rather as a transformational guide.

It is my hope that you be validated by what you read as well as motivated to produce change that fosters results for the hundreds of very deserving students within your school.

ix

KEY CONCEPTS

"How wonderful it is that nobody need wait a single moment before starting to improve the world."

— Anne Frank

1 For some children, the only hope to escape a life of poverty is found through the front gates of a school that cares.

2 The humble beginnings of Damen and his family acted as a driving force for change.

3 The words "After high school comes college" shaped the author's view on education, and instilled in him a passion to influence the lives of others through the work of the No Excuses University.

FIVE WHISPERED WORDS

I had watched hundreds of children walk through the gates of our campus each day in my six years as the principal of Los Peñasquitos Elementary School, but this one child was different. At the time I didn't know exactly what led me to follow him to his classroom, but as I reflect back on that day I realize that it wasn't just one thing; it might have been many. Maybe it was the tattered clothes that he was wearing. His white tank top t-shirt and cutoff jeans, covered in dirt stains, was the most unlikely first-day-of-school outfit that someone could imagine. Maybe it was the way his mother walked beside him as his younger sister held on to her dress and his baby brother was being transported on her back as is the custom in their Mixteco culture. Or maybe it was the butcher's bag that was dangling from his left hand, holding a sippy cup of milk and a small snack wrapped in aluminum foil. This bag that you and I throw away after so many visits to the grocery store was the only semblance of a lunch sack that this little boy had on his very first day of school. Whatever it was, I knew that I had to follow him, little Aquileo, to class to find out more.

We've seen it hundreds of times. Children are brought to the door of their first kindergarten classroom with much trepidation on the part of parents. Some of the children cry as they cling to their mothers, while others walk silently into the unknown as they take seats at their places on the carpet. Little Aquileo did neither. With a huge smile on his face, he said goodbye to his mother in his native language and eagerly responded to his teacher's direction to take a seat on the orange square with his name on it. I stood there. I watched him. I could not leave. Here was a child of poverty who could not speak a word of English, yet whose bright and eager eyes told a story of hope that could fill the pages of this book. It was as if he knew that he was beginning a journey that day that had the potential to change his life forever. That day, Aquileo was a reminder of my purpose as an educator, because that day he reminded me of … me. Thirty-four years ago, my life started under similar circumstances. And while I would never know the depths of poverty the way that young Aquileo would, I do remember the times that I clearly stood out as the exception rather than the rule.

I grew up about an hour and a half outside the city of San Diego in the small mountain town of Julian. This one-stop-sign community has grown since we moved there in 1976 (it now has two stop signs), but at the time it was called home by a little more than a thousand people. Because of the rural environment of the town, there weren't many housing options for families who couldn't afford to purchase a home. In fact, the only available apartment we could find at the time was on the second floor of the Julian Market. It wasn't spacious, nor was it clean, but it did bring the perks that could only be found by a family who had nowhere to go but up. One of those perks was to spend each night cleaning the store in exchange for an extra $50 a month off the rent. Every night, my parents, brother, and I would go downstairs and do our best version of "whistle while you work." My mom, Barbara, would sweep, my dad, Steve, would mop, and my brother, Dan, and I, were taught to arrange the cans on the shelves just right so that the labels would always be facing out. Truth be told, it wasn't long before our version of *stocking* turned into *stacking* and my parents soon realized that we weren't exactly expediting the cleaning process. But because we were doing our best, and because there was no one to watch us while they worked, my parents insisted on having us participate.

In the afternoons as the sun went down, my brother and I would retreat next door to an empty parking lot to play with a group of kids that lived close by. This was the hangout where the rule "no shoes, no shirts" did not exist. During the weekday afternoons, we would ride bikes and walk the trails throughout the small town. Occasionally we would witness a drunk who was a bit out of hand or a fight between two locals whose lives, and wives, had crossed paths in all of the wrong ways the night before. As we observed the colorful characters within our community, we grew up finding normalcy amid what by many accounts would be seen as atypical to families who valued social and academic success. As I look back, I now know that unlike Aquileo, I was not growing up in a cycle of generational poverty. I was experiencing an example of situational poverty. I also understand why my parents were so motivated to exit us out of these circumstances as fast as they could.

My father did so by working any job that he could in order to pay the bills in the short term. He would sit on the steps of the grocery store every morning and ask the construction foremen if they needed an extra helper for the day. When asked by a contractor if he knew how to _____ (fill in the blank), he would exclaim with confidence that he was highly skilled. Electrician or butcher, carpenter or logger, my father never pushed away work. His commitment to his family was just too great to exhibit any kind of pride that might stand in the way of putting dinner on the table.

Much like my father, my mother did everything in her power to support the family. I never knew it then, but her pride was also challenged in her daily life. No example is greater than the times that we would walk to the post office on Sundays in order to get free bread, milk, and cheese. At the time, my brother and I thought that we must have hit the dairy lottery. Later however, we found out that those free handouts were an example of government welfare that my family had no choice but to partake in. In hindsight, such participation on the part of my mom and dad never skewed our pride in them. Instead, it has helped us to develop an understanding of the source of my mother's motivation to "break the cycle," as she would say, of a status-quo life for each of us. And in spite of the fact that neither of my parents were college educated, they operated with an understanding of just how important it would be for us to be. Proof of this came in the form of our nightly bedtime routine.

Every evening, no matter the circumstances that transpired during the day, the family ritual in that little apartment remained the same. My mom would tuck my brother and me into bed, read us a story, pat us on the chest, and whisper the words "after high school comes college" in our ears. These same words that my mother shared with me as a young boy just so happened to be some of the first words that little Aquileo would hear from his teacher on the day that he entered his kindergarten classroom for the first time. Little did I know the impact they would make on me decades later and perhaps on Aquileo decades from today. What started as a whisper from the mouth of my mother has now become a rally cry for educators across this country as they promote college readiness through what is known as the No Excuses University endeavor. And while we now know the origin of its beginning, it is up to you to define just how far this work of promoting college readiness will go. It is my hope that motivation for this cause will be found by you in this book. May it inspire you to provide never-ending hope for our neediest children.

CHAPTER ONE

THEORY TO PRACTICE

ITEMS FOR ARTICULATION

❏ Take the time to share with your colleagues thoughts about the person or persons in your life who helped to break a chain of events that otherwise might have led you down the wrong path.

❏ Who is your Aquileo? What evidence do you have that the work being done within your classroom and school is offering ways to break the cycle of poverty for kids like him?

ITEMS FOR ACTION

❏ On a blank piece of paper, create a checklist of reservations that you may have in promoting college readiness to students. For example, some may feel that students in elementary school are too young to understand, while others may be concerned that the parent community will lack support for such an endeavor. Whatever your concerns, write them down. When you are done, put the paper in a small, sealed envelope and place it at the back of the book. You'll be asked to revisit your concerns later on in your reading.

KEY CONCEPTS

"Don't wait for extraordinary opportunities. Seize common occasions and make them great. Weak men wait for opportunities; strong men make them."

— Orison Swett Marden

1 Many will have you believe that the process of change is much harder than it actually is … don't believe them.

2 Acting with a spirit of mindful risk-taking is often much more productive than waiting on sloth-like research studies that may or may not exist.

3 Because of an impatient obsession to achieve academic success, the Los Pen staff chose to BE the research and find new ways to promote college readiness for all students.

LET'S BE THE RESEARCH

December 20, 2003. I remember this night the same way I do the birthdates of my children. Shuffling in the dark, I woke up searching for something to write on in an effort to document the kind of inspiration that seems to come only in the middle of the night. As a relatively new principal, I had learned to always keep a notepad and pen on my nightstand for times just like these, but on this night I couldn't find either. Not wanting to lose my thought, I turned on the lights in desperation, waking my wife and our brand-new baby. Immediately, I scribbled the words "Let's BE the research!" on a 4x6 lined notepad. These words, which lacked the slightest significance to my wife at the time, would eventually launch an endeavor that is changing the lives of children across the country. But before you understand their meaning, you must first understand the inspiration behind them.

In September 2002, I found myself packed into the superintendent's meeting room alongside two dozen elementary school principals from all over our district. Cabinet members greeted each of us with a hope that sprung eternal after a well-deserved summer break. In turn I, like so many of my colleagues, entered this first administrative meeting with an eagerness to welcome a new year the way a painter does a blank canvas.

As was always the case, the agenda for the morning was broken up into two distinct categories. The first were the housekeeping items that brought an abundance of minutiae and ensured that our role as *managers* was secure. The second was based on the district's yearly strategic plan. This portion of the agenda intended to encourage us as *leaders* who actively sought ideas and strategies in the hope that we would create greater academic and social success for our students. I had been through meetings like these on a number of occasions, and to be honest with you, they rarely if ever inspired me as a leader. However, on this day I was hopeful that the message might be different. To my surprise, it was.

The members of the superintendent's cabinet stood strategically around the room as one of our top district leaders shared the number one goal of our district. "This year, the number one initiative of our district is to promote college readiness for all!" he said excitedly.

I watched the faces of my colleagues as we all eagerly

waited to hear more information. Silence. That was it. After a few brief seconds, sensing that I was not alone in my question, I stood up and asked, "What does that mean for elementary school?"

This very fair question immediately received a very fair response, which was, "We don't know. We haven't done the research. We're going to learn a lot more this year."

Accepting this answer as one that was more than reasonable, we concluded the meeting and went on our way.

After a year went by, I found myself in that same room, with that same group of elementary school principals. Again, the proclamation was made: "The number one goal of our district is to promote college readiness for all."

Again, I asked the same question. "What does that mean for elementary school?"

This time, the answer was different, but far more disappointing. "We don't quite know because we really couldn't find the research," said the cabinet member.

As the meeting wrapped up on that fall day, I left with a great sense of frustration over the lack of direction that was given to us as leaders. And while I found the mission of college readiness to be one that was noble, I didn't exactly believe that what my district was stating was all that creative. This to me was a perfect example of setting a lofty goal without offering a means to achieve it. It's safe to say that this likely was not my district leadership's intention, but it did nonetheless cause great frustration for me and my colleagues alike. In fact, I found myself frustrated by this lack of direction for months. Which brings me back to that early morning in December.

The clock read 2 a.m. and I was the only one in my house who was not fast asleep. I stared at the ceiling for many minutes before finally writing down those four life-changing words: "Let's BE the research!" Unlike the times where I processed a thought over and over again before writing it down, these words were immediate and demanded action. I remember thinking to myself, "Damen, get this on paper. Something big is about to happen!"

Whether it was my desire to share my inspiration or simply my need to explain why I had turned on the lights in the middle of the night, I made my wife sit up in our bed and listen to what I had to say. "Lara, Lara, you've got to listen to this. I've got a great…"

Before any more words could leap from my mouth to her ears, she grabbed me by the cheeks, looked affectionately in my eyes, and said, "Damen, go back to sleep and leave me alone!"

I couldn't blame her for wanting to go back to bed, but I insisted that she needed to hear me out. I exclaimed, "No Lara, you don't understand. I have a great idea and I have to process it with someone. Just listen."

Sensing that her attention span was not capable of keeping up with my excitement, she convinced me to take my ideas into our small home office and get my thoughts on paper. For six hours I sat at my computer writing notes, listing bullet points, and laying out a plan that I believed had the ability to revolutionize public education. Soon after 8 a.m., my wife walked into our office, took a seat at a chair, and said, "I'm ready to listen."

I won't lie to you when I share that I looked at her with tears in my eyes and said, "There's a lot to do and I need to work closely with my staff on this, but I think I just found a way to change the lives of thousands of children across this country."

Before I could speak another word, my wife looked at me and said, "I don't know what you are going to tell me, but I can tell by the look in your eyes that you are telling me the truth."

I indeed was that morning when I spoke with my wife and I certainly am today as I write for you. What began so randomly in the middle of the night has become a systematic endeavor that is changing the lives of thousands of students, educators, and families across this country. That endeavor acts not only as the title of this book, but more importantly as a renewed sense of hope for even our most challenged students.

The No Excuses University was founded in January 2004

with the support of the Los Peñasquitos Elementary School staff. After being told by many that the most successful initiatives were ones that required the approval of academics who conducted research studies on efficacy, our staff boldly decided to go about our business in a unique way. We decided that instead of waiting for the results of studies that were not even being conducted, we would become the research. Such experimental reform is often looked at as careless by those who embrace the status quo, but for our staff it's really all we've known for more than a decade. Unfortunately, I remember a time when this positive entrepreneurial spirit was all but non-existent at our school.

CHAPTER TWO

THEORY TO PRACTICE

ITEMS FOR ARTICULATION

❏ Think about a time when your school was told that something could not be done because of a lack of resources, research, personnel, etc. How did you handle this problem? Did you give up, or did you find a way to create success in spite of such challenges?

ITEMS FOR ACTION

❏ As a team, think about one strategy, lesson, unit, or intervention that you have been putting off creating because of a lack of resources or research. Make a plan today to go forward collaboratively and implement this one idea.

KEY CONCEPTS

"We are all faced with a series of great opportunities brilliantly disguised as impossible situations."

— Charles Swindoll

1 One goal was created: Every student without exception and without excuses will be proficient in reading, writing, and math.

2 Six exceptional systems helped to transform Los Pen from the lowest performing school in its district to one of the highest performing schools in the state of California.

3 The exceptional system staircase helps to guide schools within the No Excuses University Network.

FINDING POSSIBLE IN THE IMPOSSIBLE

While performing at the Lincoln Center in New York City, Itzhak Perlman, renowned as one of the best violinists ever to play, encountered a challenge unlike anything experienced by the crowd or him before. After playing just a few bars of a solo, the audience heard a loud twang and snap that came from Perlman's violin. The nightmare of a broken string had come during the playing of Mendelssohn's Violin Concerto, a piece that many had deemed impossible to play. Because Perlman suffers from the effects of polio, a disease he has battled since he was a child, he did not get up to replace his instrument, as is the custom during such a time. Instead, silence blanketed the crowd as he paused and then began to play with the three remaining strings. In spite of such a great challenge, it is said that he played the remainder of the arrangement flawlessly.

Afterward he was asked how he was able to accomplish such a tremendous feat. Perlman simply replied, "You know, sometimes it is the artist's task to find out how much music you can still make with what you have left."

Just as Itzhak Perlman found success in what others deemed to be impossible, so too must educators as they work with a wide array of students. In 1995, I started my career at Los Peñasquitos Elementary School as a one-on-one special support teacher for a student who was struggling with his behavior. I didn't know much about the school, known as "Los Pen" by those in the community, other than that it was the lowest performing in the Poway Unified School District, which is 25 minutes outside the city of San Diego. Before accepting the job, I conducted some informal research and asked several teachers whom I knew around the district for their advice. There seemed to be a universal agreement that this was the place that, as one teacher told me, "Good careers go to die."

"It's the lowest performing school in the district and it always will be," said one person.

"That's the place where all of the poor, second-language students and drug-addicted parents live," said another.

No matter how hard I tried to encourage a nice word to be said about this place, there were none to be found. Still, I accepted the position with the idea that I could always leave if I chose to do so. As I think back, it's amazing I lasted more than a day.

Jason was a third-grade student who battled OCD (obsessive-compulsive disorder) as well as a mild form of Tourette's syndrome. Told that he was a good boy at his core, I introduced myself to him one early morning. My job was clearly defined as "Jason's special teacher," which in layman's terms meant that I was responsible for keeping him out of trouble and on task. I soon found that Jason had no "get to know you" phase; he immediately showed a side of himself that explained why he required individual attention in the first place. While many felt that Jason made the choice to disobey the rules, the fact was that his lack of ability to process simple directions made it difficult for him to manage in the classroom without help. When he didn't get what he wanted, he would throw chairs and desks and he would yell at me. If he were really angry, he would hold his scissors in his hand and threaten to stab me with them. However, almost immediately after tirades like these, this third grader's conscience and tender heart would shine through. He would look me in the eyes, say he was sorry, and then on many occasions he would wrap his arms around me and hug me. As the year progressed, I found that Jason would hug me more and try to stab me less. His academic and social success became a reason for celebration for the school, his parents, and me. As I watched him mature over the next several years, this young man, who would grow up to attend Purdue University, taught me something that would stick with me for the rest of my career: *The potential of an individual student is limited only by the desire for an adult to draw upon it.* I would soon find out, however, that this lesson was not one learned, or at least believed, by a number of staff members at Los Pen.

After finishing my work with Jason, I was offered a position as a fourth-grade teacher some three doors down from the third-grade classroom that I worked in. Because I was a late hire, I had but two days to get my classroom ready for the school year. New key in hand, I opened the door that would become my very first home as a teacher. A flip of the light switch allowed fluorescent attention on what was by all accounts a gloomy setting. The desks were stacked at the back of the room and the chairs were scattered in a pile without rhyme, reason, or unified color, for that matter. In fact, the chairs of this fourth-grade classroom appeared to be a size more appropriate for our first-grade friends across the hall. The textbooks were ragged and ripped, and the teacher's desk was wobbly no matter how you arranged it. Cushy teacher's chair? As my Italian grandfather would say, "forgettaboutit!"

As I look back on that day, I realize that the lack of equitable supplies found in my room had little to do with bad luck and everything to do with the fact that my colleagues had taken the best of best and given me the leftovers. Even though I had been the victim of this pervasive form of hazing that takes place in schools across the country, my attitude remained steadfast and spirited. One of the reasons for this had to do with the voices that I heard across the hall from me.

I had been told for several months that the staff at Los Pen was one that could sometimes be challenging to work with. And while I did spend many months working as a long-term substitute, I hadn't been given the opportunity to truly work collaboratively with my colleagues in a way that would allow me to create an opinion of my own. As I heard the voices of two teachers in the room next to me, I immediately decided that the negative publicity must have been unjustified. I heard two colleagues who were actively engaged in lesson planning that was the model of collaboration. So inspired was I, that I reached into a bag of items I had bought at a local teacher supply store, pulled out my brand-new red lesson plan book, and confidently trotted to the room next door. I introduced myself, saying, "Hi, my name is Damen and I'm the new fourth-grade teacher. I see that you are planning and I'd like to join you."

After some pleasantries were exchanged, one of the teachers looked up from her chair and said, "Thanks for your offer, but we don't really *team* here; we *partner*."

Because it didn't take long for me to translate the meaning of her message, I smiled and began to walk out of the room. Before I could take my first step outside the door, the other teacher exclaimed, "By the way, your partner is right next door to you. Her name is Sandra."

A slight chuckle echoed into the hallway as I left. Even though this should have been a clear signal not to forge a partnership with Sandra, against my better judgment I opened the green accordion door that separated our two rooms.

Sandra *(whose name has been changed to protect the guilty)* was a teaching veteran of 20-plus years. It must be said that in the years since I entered the field of education, I have met many exceptional educators with 20, 30, or even 40 years of experience. In addition, I have been inspired not only by their knowledge of the curriculum but in their ability to change and seek the best new methods of teaching possible. That said, Sandra was not one of them. In fact, one of the first things that I noticed about her was that she had stacks of worksheets lined up throughout the room. With some of them dating back to the early 1970s, the worksheets clearly did not represent cutting-edge pedagogy. After seeing this, I glanced at a lesson plan book that lay lifeless on her desk. Instead of stating the days of the week or specific dates on the calendar, Sandra's book was clearly labeled "Day 1, Day 2 … Day 180." Knowing that this likely meant that her routine was set in stone, the hairs on the back of my neck began to stand up as a signal for me to shut the door and go about my own business. Again however, against my better judgment, I looked her in the eyes and timidly said, "Hi, I'm Damen and … I guess … I'm your new teaching partner."

In an instant I watched what started as a blank stare on her face turn to frustration. Immediately she scowled and said, "Partner? Partner? I don't have a partner."

I tried to explain that our colleagues had sent me over to speak to her, but it was too late; I had struck a nerve. She continued, "I've been working here for 20 years without a partner and I'm not going to start now. I'm happy to share any ideas and you are more than welcome to copy some of my worksheets, but I'm not going to partner with you."

After her declaration, she shut the accordion door and, I can only assume, went back to her work. Rejected by someone whom even others did not wish to work with, I stood stunned. While it was many years ago, I vividly remember sitting in a pea-soup green, kindergarten-size chair in the middle of the room, saying to myself, "Damen, what the hell did you get yourself into?"

Even though I would take great joy in teaching the wonderful students who made up my very first class, I must say that I survived that year on will alone. Unfortunately, by the end of the second year, I had turned into someone whom I grew to despise.

For years I had heard excuses from educators about why some students could not learn. Whether it was because their kids were poor, spoke a different language, or had parents who just didn't care, I made it a point to turn my back on colleagues who displayed such negative attitudes. Little did I know, however, that I would begin to take that same path. After teaching for two years, I soon discovered how hard it was to teach students with challenges, especially those who lived in poverty. After months of fighting inner frustrations, I remember being in the staff lounge and sharing with a colleague about one of my students. "What the heck am I supposed to do when this kid's parents don't even read with him at home!" I exclaimed.

In an effort to comfort me, my colleague said, "Welcome to the club."

As he said it, he took a certain sense of joy in the statement that made me uncomfortable. Later, I walked through the hallways asking myself, "Is this really a club that you want to be in?"

The answer to this was clearly "no," and I had decided then and there that I would rather give up a profession that I was passionate about than to become another example of status-quo teaching. I had decided that I would pursue another line of work at the end of the year. Fortunately for me, I never had to make that choice because, in many ways, a different choice was made for me.

Jeff King was assigned as the new principal of Los Peñasquitos Elementary School at the end of my second year. I didn't know much about him, and had only heard that he was someone who was passionate about changing the reputation and results of Los Pen. So, convinced about his potential as a leader by the reputation that preceded him, I decided I needed to stick around and see what kind of changes would be made for the better. To this day, it is one of the best professional decisions I have ever made.

Jeff was bold, fearless, and sometimes brash, but he was just what the doctor ordered for a school that had been failing for decades. From the first moment that Jeff spoke to our staff, until the day that he left Los Pen some five years later and I replaced him as the principal, he never wavered from his expectations of us as professionals. With Jeff, there was but one goal: *Every student, without exception and without excuse, will be proficient or advanced in reading, writing, and math.* It was that simple. What started as an edict from Jeff's lips to our ears became a motivational mantra that still exists today. This unlikely goal, from a school where four in ten students live in poverty, stands today not because it sounds good or is inspirational. It still exists today because it works!

Los Peñasquitos Elementary School is made up of 650 students representing 35 different languages. Forty-two percent of our kids live in poverty, most residing within the largest Section 8 subsidized housing complex in Northern San Diego County. Crime levels and drug use are the highest in our district. There's no doubt that such demographics have acted as a tailor-made excuse for our school's poor performance over the years. With challenges like these, poor performance was not only acceptable within our district; it was expected. Because of this, many might suggest that setting a goal with academics at the forefront was an exercise in futility. Our fundamental belief in all students, however, would drastically change those perceptions and foster results that would make Los Pen a showcase for schools across the nation to follow.

Between 1997 and 2008, our school went from being the laughing stock of our community to the darling of Title I schools in the state of California. The staff at Los Pen worked

27

diligently to promote academic success for every student, no matter the circumstance. As a result of their commitment, our school was ranked within the top ten percent of all schools in the state of California six times between 2001 and 2008. In addition, Los Pen was ranked number one out of 100 similar schools in our state for three consecutive years. While schools similar to ours were challenged to find academic results that closed the achievement gap between subgroups, each of Los Pen's five subgroups met levels of academic success that exceeded the norm. The focus of research studies, books, magazine articles, and news reports, Los Peñasquitos Elementary has created a momentum for change that is affecting the lives of thousands of students across the United States. Schools with far more challenging demographics than ours, which you'll read about later in this book, have found similar success by following the six exceptional systems created by the staff of Los Peñasquitos Elementary School.

Six Exceptional Systems

As written about in the book *TurnAround Schools: Creating Cultures of Universal Achievement*, by Jeff King and me, the secret to our school's success is in the simplicity of our systems. These six systems are working to shift the culture of schools across the country as they help to generate academic results for even the most challenging demographics within a school's student population.

Culture of Universal Achievement

When you boil it down, a culture of universal achievement is about the beliefs that adults hold toward the students they teach. No matter the challenges faced by a school, it is essential for every staff member to believe in the academic potential of each student. In addition, every adult on campus must also understand that it is his or her responsibility to translate that potential into reality. In the end, it all comes down to belief. What do you believe?

No matter where I go or whom I speak with, someone always wants to know why this concept of belief is so important. To me, it's actually very simple. When you believe in something with all of your heart, it changes your behavior. When you believe in your marriage, it changes the way you work with your spouse when problems arise. When you believe in your children, it changes the way you parent them. When you believe in your students and their potential, it changes the way you teach. It changes the way you respond to their individual needs. I must be candid with you. If you don't believe in the potential of your students, you may find it very difficult to find value in this book. That is because there is nothing that can be found in future chapters that will ever replace this paramount virtue of belief. It's that important.

Collaboration

There is a difference between a group and a team. Groups show up at the same time, in the same place. Teams show up to meet at the same time, in the same place, with a specific purpose. The purpose of teams that truly collaborate is always to focus on new, better, data-driven ways to impact student learning. True collaboration exists when teams make collective commitments to finding breakthroughs in learning and sharing them with one another on a regular basis.

STANDARDS ALIGNMENT

Let's face it; aligning your teaching to state standards lacks a sense of educational romance, if you will. In fact, it is often described as the trenches of teaching. Belaboring as it may be to some, it is critical for the overall success of a school. Unfortunately, there are those who think that aligning one's standards is simply a matter of opening a textbook and following the pacing guide. I saw this firsthand while working with a school in the spring of 2008.

Just as I began my presentation on the importance of standards alignment, a young teacher stood up and said, "I don't mean to be rude, but you're in Texas, where we invented standards alignment."

I smiled on the outside because of her sweet demeanor, but cringed on the inside because of her misguided attitude. She continued, "Do we really need to be here if we've already done it?"

I said to her candidly, "Standards alignment is not something that you've **done**; it's something that you **do**."

I wanted this teacher and her colleagues to understand that the greatest learning, and joy as a teacher, cannot be found in the completion of mapping out the standards for any given year. It is found in the journey that allows you to discover new, better strategies to align your work as a grade level and hence create better results for your students on a regular basis.

Plan for Assessment

When a team collaborates around curriculum that is aligned to the standards, they must then decide how to assess their success. I'm always amazed at the lack of continuity that exists in the area of carefully selected common assessments between grade levels. When a team fails to create and select common assessments, there can be no credible dialogue between them. It is essential that a school selects assessments that have the ability to drive instruction for the individual student. One example of such an assessment is the Measures of Academic Progress (MAP) assessment created by the Northwest Evaluation Association.

MAP testing allows students to complete an assessment online and receive immediate feedback. Teachers can then take this information in the areas of reading, language, math, and science, and find the strengths and areas of need for each individual student. All of these assessments, which can be given from kindergarten to eighth grade, align to individual state standards. Such a test is invaluable; it not only specifies learning needs for the individual student, but also creates unity in assessment from one grade level to the next.

DATA ANALYSIS

As 35 languages are represented within the student body of Los Pen, I am often asked, "What is the most commonly spoken language at your school?" I love this question because it allows me to give one of my favorite answers. I always respond, "The most commonly spoken language at our school is data."

Our staff speaks the language of data. We communicate with our parents through the use of data. And, most importantly, we teach our students the value of data. In fact, every single student at Los Pen, as well as at many No Excuses University schools across the country, creates individual goals based on very specific data. I never truly understood the value of this until I met Emerson.

Emerson was a third-grade student whose native language was Tagalog. I watched this spunky young student skipping through the hallways one day on his way to recess. Even though the huge smile on his face was a common feature for him, I wanted to know if there was any special reason for his spirited attitude on this specific day. I stopped him and said, "Hi Emerson, how are you doing today?"

Immediately he responded with "Great!" and then attempted to be on his way.

Not content with his response, I said, "Wait a minute. How do you know you're doing great?"

He paused for a moment, looked up at me, and said, "I know I'm doing great because I just got a 198 on my MAP score. And do you know what's so great about that Mr. Lopez?"

"No," I said.

Emerson shouted back with excitement, "What's so great about that is that I made the most growth in my goal area, which is in literal comprehension. If I keep it up, I will be past grade level and I'll be ready to make a new goal."

So pleased with him, I gave Emerson a high five and sent him on his way. After he left, I beamed with pride for Emerson and also for his outstanding teacher who understood the value of creating a student-teacher partnership focused on a common language of data.

INTERVENTIONS

A few years back, I took my family on a trip to Portland. (Driving from San Diego to the Pacific Northwest with three small children is an adventure that could take up a whole chapter!) As we drove along the Oregon coast, I noticed a series of logging trucks driving in the opposite direction with enormous loads of perfectly cut-down trees. After seemingly hundreds of trucks passed by, I thought to myself, "How do they cut down those huge trees so perfectly?"

During our next stop for gas, I was so intrigued that I went up to an elderly gentleman who was a local resident in the area. I asked him, "How do they cut down those trees so perfectly and make the most of the wood?"

As it turns out, this gentleman had worked in the industry for a number of years and by the lengthy answer that I received, I could tell that he loved to talk about the process. He told me, "First we used an ax and a two-man saw. After that, the chainsaw came along and made life a lot easier for us."

He went on. "While they still use a chainsaw, there's now a machine that makes everything as easy as can be. This 'tree-tractor' has a jaw that clamps to the trunk of the tree. As it clamps, it takes a measurement of the circumference of the tree and sends it to a computer inside the tractor where the operator sits. This circumference measurement tells the machine the approximate height of the tree and a chainsaw that is attached to the clamp cuts down the tree and systematically slices it into sections that maximize board length."

I was amazed. "All because of one measurement?"

"That's right," he said. "All because of one measurement."

I have found a direct correlation between this method of cutting down trees and a school's desire to provide data-driven interventions. Good schools are able to take *interventions* and analyze their effectiveness through the use of data. Great schools, however, are able to take *data* and translate it directly into the creation of appropriate interventions. For example, just as the tree-cutting machine took one measurement and cut the tree in a way that maximized board length, educators can take a fluency score or math assessment and plug students into appropriate interventions. At Los Pen, if a student receives a fluency score of 80, then he or she might be directed to work in our Read Naturally Lab. If a math assessment identifies a weakness in problem solving for a student, teams might offer support through six clearly identified problem-solving strategies. The best schools will look at data and say, "If *this* data—then *this* intervention." As challenging as this is, and it is, we are living in an educational environment that enables us to make such choices because of our access to exceptional assessments and interventions that align with them.

As you think about these six exceptional systems, visualize them as a staircase. At the foundation is a culture of universal achievement. When you believe in your students, you collaborate with that belief at your core. When you collaborate, you ensure that your work is aligned to standards. As you continue, you select common assessments that also align to those same standards. Data is then collected from common assessments and students are plugged into meaningful interventions that create academic results.

How many times has your school taken on too many goals or initiatives only to find none of them were successful? This staircase was developed in such a way that encourages schools to take one step at a time, get the system right, and then move on. To jump from a culture of universal achievement to interventions may create scattered success, but it will never create the kind of long-term educational prosperity that occurs when schools move systematically up the staircase.

As we work to promote college readiness for all, this exceptional system staircase acts as the core, the foundation for our endeavor. In order for the No Excuses University model to grow from one school in Southern California to dozens of schools across the nation (62 *schools as of June 2009*), our staff was dedicated to keeping true to these fundamentals. From the beginning of our journey, these six exceptional systems have represented the north of our compass, supporting the travels we've made to a destination that focuses on college readiness.

THEORY TO PRACTICE

ITEMS FOR ARTICULATION

❏ How many goals does your school have? Can you name them all? Is there one goal that stands out as a driving force for continuous improvement?

❏ On which step do you see your school on the exceptional systems staircase?

ITEMS FOR ACTION

❏ As a school, decide upon one goal that drives everything that you do. Get it in writing and live by it. If you have several goals, stop thinking of them as "goals" and start thinking of them as steps to help achieve your ONE GOAL.

❏ Use the lessons learned in the book *TurnAround Schools: Creating Cultures of Universal Achievement* to help your school begin its journey up the exceptional systems staircase.

KEY CONCEPTS

🔑

"We must accept finite disappointment, but never lose infinite hope."

— Martin Luther King, Jr.

1 Unjust assumptions rob students of hope and silence the call of an educator to create results in areas void of success.

2 Beware of educators who subscribe to a "perfection before participation" attitude.

3 When it comes to school transformation, rather than seek immediate solutions, we must embrace a "value-added" philosophy.

4 Because we cannot predict the future for a five-year-old, we have no choice but to prepare ALL students for a life that includes college.

WHAT'S THE ALTERNATIVE?

Questions are not typically common during a keynote address, but the woman in the audience just couldn't hold back. While speaking in Chicago about the importance of promoting college readiness in elementary school, I must have said something that touched a nerve. Heedless of the results that I shared and examples of how our college readiness focus is changing the lives of students, she was compelled to speak up. So she yelled from the back of the room, "Aren't you disenfranchising our kids?"

"Excuse me?" I asked.

She continued, "Many students without U.S. citizenship will finish high school just to find out that they are not allowed to attend public universities. Poor students will do the same and realize that they don't have the funds to go to college. What about them?"

It was quiet; I was stumped. After about thirty seconds of listening to a still room, I looked under the brightness of the stage lights and offered the only words that I could think of to share. "What's the alternative?"

For years, most of us have been guilty of making unjust assumptions about the students who walk through the doors of our classrooms. Children who live in generational poverty are seen as perfect candidates for low-skilled work in the future. Non-English-speaking students are assumed to have very little chance of finding professions that may some day provide financial and social stability for their future families. And minority students are often given the automatic burden that their best will never be good enough and therefore are taught by many to accept their place in society. But what is worse than all of these labels is the fact that these assumptions are branded on children at the age of four or five as they enter kindergarten. This unspoken and all too common belief, on the part of even some of our best educators, is exactly why we must take bold risks to do things differently. People who think like this audience member are reluctant to take such risks because:

They don't understand the true meaning of "college readiness": College readiness is not the belief that every student will go to college. College readiness is the idea that every student deserves the opportunity to be educated in a way that prepares him or her for college if he or she chooses to attend.

They subscribe to the theory of "perfection before participation": Many educators have been taught that thinking outside the box is a practice that is not acceptable. In addition, many watch school reforms come and go and therefore decide to dig their heels into mediocrity. No matter the case, they fall into what I call the perfection before participation trap. This trap is one that encourages educators to take part only in educational endeavors that are comprehensively perfect in every way. When a program or model is not perfect in their eyes, they eagerly find a flaw and refuse to participate. In the end, their lack of participation is not based on reflective evaluation, but rather convenient excuse-making.

They don't embrace a "value-added" philosophy: Recently, I was at a school in Arizona conducting a workshop on creating individual academic goals for students. As I shared several practical strategies with this middle school staff, one gentleman shouted out, "Are you crazy? You're in elementary school where you only have 30 kids in each class. We have 125 students to teach every day. Do you really expect for us to make individual goals for each of them?"

After trying to validate his concerns, I asked the man, "If you can't create goals with all of your students, do you think that you could do so with half of them?"

He laughed and simply said, "No."

I went on. "If I gave you a month, could you conduct them with 40 to 50 students?"

Again he shrugged off my suggestion and gave me a very solid "No!"

I asked again, "If I gave you a week, do you think you could personalize goals for two or three students?"

He convincingly smiled and said, "Of course I could do that."

I finally and firmly stated, "Then that's two or three students that have goals next week that didn't have them this week."

This is a perfect example of someone not knowing what it means to think in a "value-added" way. Too many times educators subscribe to an "all or nothing" mentality. Changing the overall results of your school is not done with one sweeping initiative; it is done by finding lots of little ways to add value to the educational lives of individual students. This same idea applies when it comes to promoting college readiness. No matter the long-term outcome, a student who is taught with a college-readiness focus is better equipped academically than one who has not been given that same preparation.

They behave like fortunetellers: The thought that the promotion of "college readiness for all" would disenfranchise students is the epitome of a very misguided assumption. While people rarely say it out loud, they often make assumptions clearly indicating that it would be better not to offer false hope to children by talking about a future that includes college. By doing so, we behave like unsolicited fortunetellers. Think about it for a moment. Should educators be expected to ignore the fact that laws can change, citizenship can be attained, and financial situations have the potential to improve over the course of the thirteen years that a student is in school? Furthermore, should we be expected to share with these same students the idea that higher education is a concept that exclusively exists within our country? This kind of thinking is absolutely absurd. Because of this, we should no longer attempt to predict the future of five-year-olds based on the color of their skin, their socioeconomic levels, or their native languages. And because we lack the ability to truly predict the future, we have no choice but to believe in every student's potential to attend an institute of higher education.

As I reflect back to that keynote speech in Chicago, I realize that the woman in the audience, and others who think like her, would have loved for me to offer the perfect solution for getting students out of poverty and into college. Or perhaps she'd be glad if I had no answers at all, for then she could continue to make herself feel better about not meeting the needs of her more challenging students. But the fact is that the business of promoting college readiness is not a perfect science, especially when you are starting in kindergarten. And while some may see it as a risky endeavor, we must decide to ignore the people in the audience who seek only perfect solutions to very challenging problems. True, these bold practices may not remove all of the roadblocks on the path to college for our most needy children, but there's no evidence that would suggest that such measures would hinder their academic potential, either. In fact, as you will read, the data suggest quite the contrary.

THEORY TO PRACTICE

ITEMS FOR ARTICULATION

❏ What are the challenges that some students face in their pursuit of a college education?

ITEMS FOR ACTION

❏ If your school stood before a jury, what evidence would you have for them to convict you of displaying confidence in every student's potential to graduate from college? As a team, seek tangible evidence to present at an upcoming staff meeting. During this time, share your team's view of the strengths and challenges that your school has when it comes to believing in all students.

CHAPTER FIVE

Key Concepts

ႁ

"If you think education is expensive, try ignorance!"

— Derek Bok

1 The value of a college education is displayed in abundance in the areas of *personal prosperity* and *societal wealth*.

2 The level to which a person is educated either drastically increases or decreases their financial, physical, and emotional wellness.

3 Single mothers without a high school education are five times more likely to live in poverty than those with a bachelor's degree.

4 There are three times as many black and Hispanic males in prison cells as there are in college dormitories.

A RATIONALE FOR READINESS

I sn't it amazing how one statistic, one injustice, or one experience in the lives of everyday people is often enough to trigger the human spirit to produce remarkable results? Such was the case with two very inspiring young men. Darius Weems was a 15-year-old boy suffering from Duchenne muscular dystrophy (DMD). As the number one genetic killer of children, this disease robs an individual of physical tools and prevents many from living to see their early 20s. Logan Smalley was a college student with a passion for supporting children with special needs and an artistic touch for filmmaking. Darius was black. Logan was white. Darius was a high school student who had never traveled outside the city limits of Athens. Logan had been accepted into Harvard grad school and was about to experience a journey well beyond the Georgia borders. This unlikely pair made a series of decisions that have touched the lives of tens of thousands of people around the globe and raised millions for DMD research in the process.

As a college student, Logan Smalley volunteered at Project Reach, a summer camp for children with disabilities. One of the attendees at the center was Darius' older brother Mario. Before Mario, a Duchenne's sufferer as well, passed away at the age of 19, he asked Logan to "watch after my little brother." The pain of watching his friend die at such a young age did not trigger in Logan depression and hopelessness the way that it does in so many others. Rather, it spurred on action. In 2004, Logan and ten of his friends set out to take Darius on a 7,000-mile road trip and film a documentary at the same time in order to raise funds for DMD research. What began as a pipedream for a dozen college-aged kids has become one of the most award-winning documentaries in recent history. The film, *Darius Goes West*, explicitly recognizes the odds that are stacked against sufferers of Duchenne's, yet chooses to defy the idea that nothing can be done about it. In 2007, this inspirational team set a goal to sell one million DVDs in one year. Some saw such a feat as completely irrational and unlikely at best. However, Logan, Darius, and their friends understood two important facts that necessitated this great sense of urgency. First, Duchenne's was a non-curable disease that was 100% fatal. Second, every day and every dollar counted.

The ability for individuals to use the data before them in

order to find unique solutions is unfortunately a very precious commodity in the world of public education. The tremendous progress that the *Darius Goes West* team has made in light of limited resources is an example that should offer perspective for what our struggles are as educators. If poverty is the illness and college is the cure, then our behavior should match that of Logan and Darius. Today, we have data about the value of college that is more than enough to generate a substantial sense of urgency for teachers and develop a cure for students at the same time.

I have worked diligently to compile an abundance of data about the value of earning a college degree. The results that I have found are overwhelming. A life accompanied by a college degree is one that is richer in ways that go well beyond finances. The potential that awaits our society when one college grad becomes a thousand and thousands become millions is staggering. I have arranged these outcomes into two specific categories: ***personal prosperity*** and ***societal wealth***. Both categories display the effect that a college education has on the life of an individual as well as those who live within our communities.

Because this book, and especially this chapter, was written with the practitioner in mind, I have created *data boxes* that clearly display the statistical facts about the value of a higher education. The sources of each data box have come from some of the best researchers and research studies in the field. Educators like Dr. Sandy Baum and Jennifer Ma, who wrote the study "Education Pays" on behalf of the College Board, offer insight on statistical predictors that are inspiring change in educators who learn about their research. Research studies such as "The Big Payoff," a report produced by the Commerce Department's Census Bureau and authored by Jennifer Cheeseman-Day and Eric Newburger, spotlight earnings estimates for those who stand to gain the most in the future—college grads.

The work of these authors, as well as others noted throughout this chapter, share common data that provide strong rationale for the charge to promote college readiness at an early age. From the significant gap that exists among minority groups to the benefits, or lack thereof, that a college education has on our citizens, the information from each of these sources should generate pause for all of us. As you read, I encourage you to make your own judgments and actively take notes on how you can apply the data to future educational decisions that are made for the students in your classroom, school, and district. Above all else, I encourage you to actively become the research. In the end, the true value of this chapter will not be found in the *knowledge* that you gain by reading the research, but by the *action* that you take after doing so.

PERSONAL PROSPERITY

In the 2007 College Board study "Education Pays," Sandra Baum and Jennifer Ma calculate that the gap between the lifetime earnings of a high school graduate and that of a college-educated individual widens dynamically over the course of a lifetime. They state, "The longer college graduates remain in the workforce, the greater the payoff to their investment in higher education" (Baum & Ma, 2007, p.11). The study projects that an individual with a bachelor's degree earns 61 percent more over a lifetime than a high school graduate, while a person with a master's degree earns a whopping 93 percent more than that same high school grad. Individuals with some college or associate's degrees earn between 19 and 28 percent more than those with high school diplomas.

YEARLY EARNING BY EDUCATION LEVEL

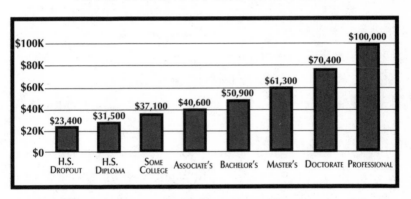

The median earnings before taxes for 25-year-olds and older indicates a 61% difference between the value of a high school diploma and a bachelor's degree.

Sources: 2006 Census Bureau; "Education Pays," 2007. Copyright © 2007, The College Board www.collegeboard.com. Reproduced with permission.

The earliest an individual can retire and collect Social Security is at the age of 62. A 25-year-old who works until he or she is 62 has a career longevity of 37 years. This means that in today's dollars an individual with a bachelor's degree would earn nearly $800,000 more in gross income in a lifetime than someone with a high school diploma. (Baum & Ma, 2007, Fig 1.2) The earnings potential of college grads becomes exponentially greater as their careers progress.

For decades, our society has blindly pitched to students an outline of education that begins in kindergarten and ends with a high school diploma. In 1970, approximately 37 percent of 18- to 19-year-olds attended college after graduating from high school (Baum & Ma, 2007). In 2007, the U.S. Department of Labor indicated that more than 67 percent, some 2 million high school graduates, were enrolled in college after graduation (Bureau of Labor Statistics, 2007). With high school dropouts generating an average income below the federal poverty level of $24,800 for a family of five (U.S. Health and Human Services, 2008), and high school graduates earning just above that, the game of life is now mandating that a college education is your ticket to personal prosperity. One can only imagine what these numbers will become when today's kindergarteners become tomorrow's high school grads. Because college has become so crucial to a person's financial and social stability, the promotion of college must start the moment students begin their educational career.

> *Sixty-nine percent of individuals with college degrees work in jobs that offer pension plans. This is 16 percent higher than that of high school graduates and 37 percent higher than high school dropouts.*

The National Longitudinal Survey of Youth reported that workers changed jobs an average of ten times between the ages of 18 and 42 (Bureau of Labor Statistics, 2006). With shifts like these, the differences between *jobs* and *careers* are becoming more defined. Many of us have experienced jobs that allowed us to pay for the basic necessities of life. I, along with so many of you, held numerous jobs throughout my days in college. From taking on serving duties with a catering company to working as a bellman at a hotel, my jobs enabled me to pay my share of the rent, fill up my gas tank, and buy food on a regular basis. Sometimes, there was just enough left over to use in a disposable fashion, but it seemed there was never enough to save for bigger and better things. As I entered the workforce as an educator, however, my monthly income from my career allowed me opportunities that my jobs never did. From being a participant in a 401K program, to the ability to purchase a new car, to a newfound opportunity to qualify for a home loan, my options became far more plentiful in a relatively short amount of time.

As we preach a life of higher education to our students,

we must remember that the benefits of a college education are found not only in a greater yearly salary, but also in our ability to participate in the vast array of benefits that a career can provide. The prospect of participation in a retirement/pension plan is a benefit that maximizes long-term financial stability to our families while minimizing undue fiscal burdens on society.

> *Highly educated individuals have a life expectancy averaging seven years longer than those who have completed a high school diploma or less.*

Source: *The Gap Gets Bigger.* 2008

In March 2008, *Health Affairs* published a study entitled "The Gap Gets Bigger: Changes in Mortality and Life Expectancy By Education" (Meara, Richards, & Cutler, 2008). The study examined both white and black men and women and offered two classifications. The first, "highly educated," was made up of individuals with some college experience. The second group was made up of the "low educated," individuals with a high school diploma or less. The authors found that highly educated individuals not only lived an average of 7 years longer than their counterparts, but also displayed a rise in life expectancy of 2.2 years between 1988 and 2000. While the life expectancy of highly educated individuals was rising, the life expectancy of low-educated adults dropped an average of 2 years in that same time span. Few would suggest that the act of sitting in a college classroom will add days to your life (many in fact would argue against such a notion); however, studies such as these offer insight into a variety of avenues by which highly educated adults can find access for greater longevity. First and foremost on that list of longevity tools is access to better health care.*The Journal of the National Cancer Institute* published a study by Dr. Ahmedin Jemal showing a decline in deaths from the four most common cancers. Within that decline, the study showed that those with 16 or more years of education benefited while those with high school diplomas or less did not. In fact, in some cases, less educated people experienced an increase in diagnoses of specific types of cancers. "Less educated people have more risk factors for cancer like smoking and obesity," said Jemal. "They receive less medical services for prevention, early detection and treatment" (Reinberg, 2008). Jemal, echoing the "Education Pays" study, noted a significant gap between college-educated adults and high school graduates when it came to both exercise habits and smoking rates. Sixty-one percent of college-educated adults between the ages of 25 and 34 exercised "vigorously," while only 31% of high school graduates did the same. By the time college graduates turned 65, they continued to out-exercise their high school counterparts by a margin of 24%. These exercise statistics, coupled with a disparity in smoking rates (9% of college-educated adults smoke compared to 26% of high school graduates), provide clear evidence of the gap in health habits based on educational levels.

No matter how you interpret these statistics, a crystal-clear argument has been made that the greater your educational background, the better access you have to quality health care. This is not to say that it is fair, nor does it suggest that quality health care is more deserved by those with higher levels of education. It simply describes a reality that exists in our society. Such information must be shared with our students as yet another reminder of the doors that are opened for those who have earned college degrees.

2006 Volunteer Rates
(52 Hours or more)

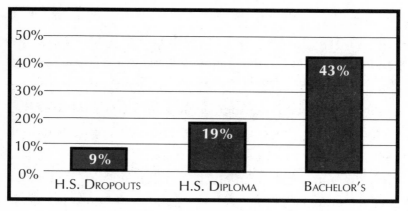

Volunteerism among college graduates is double that of high school graduates.

Source: Bureau of Labor Statistics, 2007

The significance of volunteerism cannot be overestimated. Anyone who has ever given of their time to those who are less fortunate can share about the intrinsic rewards that are gained through such participation. Unfortunately, studies show that most people do not have the time to volunteer. In fact, just more than 25% of all adults volunteer one hour a week. This statistic is dwarfed by the number of college graduates who volunteer on a regular basis. So, why is volunteerism so important? Let me offer two reasons.

First and foremost, the opportunity to volunteer is oftentimes determined by our ability to find flexibility in our schedules. Think about all of the parents in your classrooms and in your schools. Think about the ones who work in your classroom or attend field trips on a regular basis. I would wager that the majority of those who do are either in careers that offer flexibility in their schedules or parents with an income that allows one adult to stay home. I would contend from personal experience that parents who work in 9-to-5 minimum-wage jobs have far fewer opportunities to volunteer at school during the week or even in the community over the weekend. With that same experience, I could name dozens upon dozens of those same parents who wish that they could volunteer in order to spend more quality time with their children as well as to give back to the community. Their lack of participation has little to do with their drive to help others and everything to do with their ability to find flexibility in their schedules.

In addition to the joy that one finds in supporting others, volunteerism saves non-profit organizations billions of dollars annually. In 2007, the Financial Accounting Standards

Board (FASB) set the average value of a single hour of volunteering at $19.51 per hour. This figure is up 74 cents from the year before and varies from state to state (Lowest: Montana, $13.51; highest: D.C., $30.10). Think about all of the hours that you personally volunteer in your community. Tally up all of the hours that adults volunteer within your school. You do the math. The value that volunteerism has on our society is tremendous. As the data shows, the best way to raise volunteer numbers over time is to produce a college-educated workforce with a sense of stewardship for their community. Educators across our country do a wonderful job of teaching such stewardship through the development of character traits. As we teach traits aligned with volunteerism, such as citizenship and responsibility, we should remember to do so under the umbrella of a strong college-readiness message.

SOCIETAL WEALTH

In 2008, the approximately 145 million employed and 9 million unemployed made the American workforce a total of 154 million people and the average unemployment rate 5.8 percent (Bureau of Labor Statistics, 2009b). As you take a detailed look at the number of Americans who work compared to those who do not, the rationale for college readiness becomes incredibly vivid. The statistics show that roughly 62.7% of the workforce is made up of individuals with at least some college. In fact, college graduates have the largest share of the job market, making up 35% of the workforce, some 44.5 million jobs. With high school graduates making up approximately 28.5% of the American workforce, and high school dropouts following far behind as a collective 8.6%, it becomes clear that the benefits of a college education are found not only in a lower unemployment rate, but also in a higher employment ratio (Bureau of Labor Statistics, 2009b).

2008 UNEMPLOYMENT RATE
(25 YEARS OR OLDER)

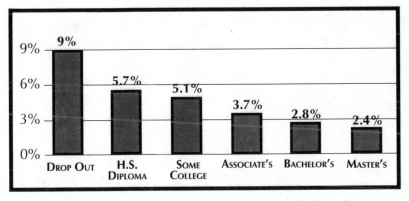

Unemployment rates are three times higher for high school dropouts than for college graduates.

Source: Bureau of Labor Statistics, 2009a

Such data flies in the face of those who would suggest that "the world needs ditch diggers too!" when in fact the world undoubtedly is seeking to hire well-educated adults. With an overwhelming number of college graduates holding the vast majority of high-paying jobs, the writing is on the wall for our students today. That writing could not be more legible for people of color, especially black students within our school system. While unemployment rates remain within the national average for whites, Asians, and Hispanics, black individuals 25 and older have a significantly higher rate than all other groups. The unemployment rate for blacks is 12.8% for those without a high school diploma and 8% for those who have graduated from high school. These numbers are double that of whites and Hispanics and nearly three times higher than that of Asians. However, with only 2.8% of *college-educated* blacks filing for unemployment benefits, this gap in employment becomes drastically reduced and far more equitable when compared to other subgroups (Baum & Ma, 2007).

These numbers have prompted many within the black community to create change with a sense of urgency that focuses on college readiness for some of the youngest children in the poorest neighborhoods. No example displays this kind of shift better than that of Geoffrey Canada and the Harlem Children's Zone.

As a child of poverty, Mr. Canada grew up in the South Bronx of New York. A graduate from the Harvard School of Education, he has maintained a steadfast commitment to improving the Harlem community for more than two decades. The Harlem Children's Zone he founded supports children and families within a 100-block area with services that help move children from a life of poverty to one of prosperity. With the Children's Defense Fund (CDF) revealing that there are nearly 1 million black children living in extreme poverty, and a reported high school dropout rate of 48%

among blacks, the challenges that were evident within the Harlem community required drastic measures. As a guest on the Oprah Winfrey show in 2007, Geoffrey Canada offered a passionate appeal for dynamic change. "Here's the problem we have in this country. We're losing kids by the tens of thousands and we are saving them by the twenties and thirties. It just doesn't add up. We have got to save these kids by the thousands."

UNEMPLOYMENT BY ETHNICITY

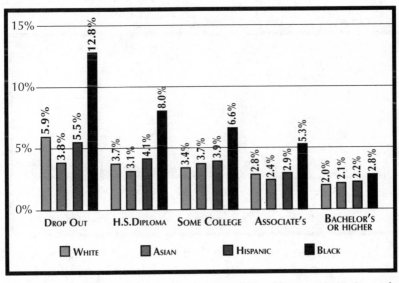

Data Provided by U.S.Department of Labor, 2007 "Education Pays," 2007. Copyright © 2007, The College Board www.collegeboard.com. Reproduced with permission.

Canada expanded on his plan to save kids. "We've got to get these kids through college. With globalization, there is nothing you can do in America with a high school diploma. These kids have got to graduate from college!"

With education at the core of the Harlem Children's Zone plan to change a community, thousands of black students are escaping the grasp of unemployment, crime, and poverty as they become college educated. Geoffrey Canada's dedication to change, as a result of the response to the negative trends within his community, provides a model for each of us to follow.

PERCENTAGE OF ADULTS LIVING IN HOUSEHOLDS OF POVERTY
(25 YEARS OR OLDER)

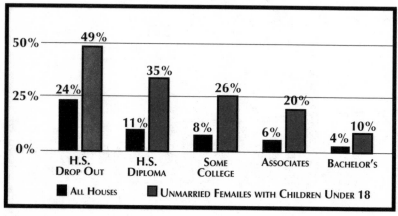

Single mothers who have dropped out of high school are nearly five times as likely to live in poverty than those with a bachelor's degree.

Source: "Education Pays," 2007. Copyright © 2007, The College Board www.collegeboard.com. Reproduced with permission.

Our students live in a world where a lack of high-paying jobs for those without college degrees will create greater financial hardships for them as individuals, and substantial burdens for all of us as a society. However, the data suggest an even greater importance for a college education when it comes to the young girls of today. As a father of four daughters, these numbers hit close to home.

To think that a single mother without a high school diploma has a 50/50 chance of living in poverty is not only worrisome; it is alarming. The number of children and single mothers who live in poverty doesn't even begin to compare with the rest of society until a college degree is obtained. If we were to view poverty as a disease, this would be a virus of epidemic proportions.

Experts offer many valid reasons for these statistics that range from the absence of fathers in the home to the need to curb teenage pregnancy. The breakdown of a parent's responsibility to his or her children is certainly one reason that has the potential to devastate the overall success of a family. Still, the greatest prescription for this problem is not necessarily to find ways to develop greater responsibility in fathers, although that doesn't hurt, but more so to establish a greater percentage of college-educated women in our society.

In "Women in the Workforce," an article by Peter Rupert and Cara Stepanczuk, the authors cite many gains in the area of employment for women that are worthy of being celebrated. From an increase in pay to a rise in level of education, women have experienced sharp improvement related to their careers over the past 25 years. With women making up approximately 48% of the workforce, however, the greatest change needed is to generate high-paying jobs for females, especially those who are single parents. The data suggest that the best way to both exit women from a life of poverty and break the cycle that perpetuates itself for generations is to increase the number of women with college degrees. This becomes increasingly important for minority women, especially black women.

Based on 2006 U.S. Census data, authors Dr. Sandy Baum and Jennifer Ma state in "Education Pays," "Median earning for Black female bachelor's degree recipients between ages 25-34 were 70% higher than median earnings for Black female high school graduates. For Hispanic women, the earnings premium was 57%, and for White women it was 49%." These numbers suggest that the only escape from poverty for a single black mother of three is via some type of post-secondary education. Because of this, our college readiness efforts must be drastically stepped up for all people of color, especially women. Such efforts cannot be expected to begin in high school; they must start in kindergarten.

The burdens of poverty not only shape a challenging existence for our children, but also stifle greater financial prosperity for our society. As you will see, the costs of Medicaid, school lunches, and the Supplemental Nutritional Assistance Program (formerly referred to as food stamps) leave the American taxpayer with monthly bills in the billions. As I share this data, do not mistake my desire for a life of personal financial responsibility for all with our call as a society to help those gripped by poverty. Let me be very clear,

PERCENTAGE OF ADULTS LIVING IN HOUSEHOLDS PARTICIPATING IN PUBLIC ASSISTANCE PROGRAMS
(25 YEARS OR OLDER)

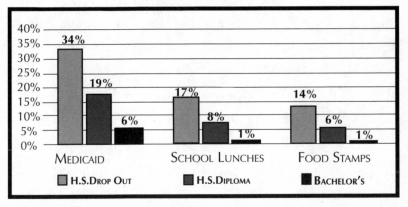

College graduates are three times less likely to participate in Medicaid, eight times less likely to have children participating in free school lunches, and six times less likely to participate in food stamps programs than high school graduates.

Sources: U.S. Census Bureau; "Education Pays," 2007. Copyright © 2007, The College Board, www.collegeboard.com. Reproduced with permission.

I believe that it is our duty to support those less fortunate, especially the children in our society who have little say in the matter. However, as we lend that support, there must be a plan to reduce an individual's long-term dependence on government aid. I believe that a systematic college-readiness endeavor, like the No Excuses University, has the potential to ensure that more children living in poverty will become college educated. As they do, a generational cycle of poverty will become broken and in turn more tax savings and revenue will be created by an increased workforce. As more dollars are saved in a reduction of welfare programs, more money can be invested in education, which will create a more positive generational cycle of success. I'll admit that such thinking may be seen as nothing more than a "pie in the sky" theory to some. True, the complexities of changing a society of more than 300 million people are so massive that it is hard to find simple solutions found within the pages of one book, but indulge me if you will as we move from the millions to one individual child at a time.

The United States Department of Agriculture (USDA) reports that more than 25.7 million people participated in the Supplemental Nutritional Assistance Program (SNAP) at a cost of $28.6 billion per month in 2005. This average monthly supplement is up more than $13 billion from 1990, with an average SNAP allotment of $1,113 per individual. As a nation we have seen participation in this program grow from 4.3 million participants a month in 1970 to more than 32.5 million participants in 2009. Such statistics go hand in hand with the drastic decline in high school graduation rates seen among people of color. When will it end? When will we as a country decide that our so-called "solutions" are not reversing this negative trend? Albert Einstein's famous definition of insanity as "doing the same thing over and over again and expecting different results" could not be more appropriate.

Medicaid, not to be confused with Medicare, is a health care program that is run by each individual state based on a list of federal guidelines. The federal and state government split the cost of health care subsidies to individuals who qualify. In 2005, almost 53 million people participated (Vock, 2006). Children make up nearly half of all individuals participating in the program, with low-income working parents, disabled Americans, and the elderly making up the rest. With the rising cost of health care for all Americans, the $330 billion-plus spent in 2005 on Medicaid is guaranteed to go up. Because the vast majority of this program serves the interests of children, it's hard to make an argument against such support. I'll be the first to say that my ability to understand the intricate nature of the politics of health care in a way that can truly promote meaningful change is like my six-month-old being able to play Mozart on the piano. Even so, it's hard to deny the data behind the significantly lower numbers of college-educated individuals who participate in this aid compared to the high school graduates who do.

Finally, when it comes to public assistance programs, the support of free or reduced breakfast and lunch for students is one that is among our noblest as a society. Regardless of your opinions of the parents who raise these children, it is our moral obligation to feed our students while they are in our care. In addition, we must never use their lack of nutrition as an excuse for poor results in school. How many times have you heard someone say, "How can we expect that kid to learn when his mother won't even feed him a good breakfast?" Decades ago, venting frustration over this may have been acceptable, but today we know better.

In 2007, the per-student funding for school lunches was $238 a year (Baum & Ma, 2007). With the more than 30 million children participating in the National School Lunch Program comes a price tag of $8.7 billion a year (USDA, 2008). Increasing from $3.7 billion in 1990 to $6.1 billion in 2000, the cost of this program is rising at a rate that is beyond the average annual U.S. inflation rate of 3%. Much like the issue of health care, a quick fix does not appear to be in the cards. Rather, a long-term approach to break the cycle of poverty through a college education is the more realistic solution.

As stated in a report by the Alliance for Excellent Education, "Crime Doesn't Pay—Diplomas Do," from the costs associated with loss of wages on the part of victims to the skyrocketing cost of incarcerating criminals, crime has become our country's greatest burden on society.

> *Seventy-five percent of state prison inmates, sixty-nine percent of jail inmates, and fifty-nine percent of federal prison inmates are high school dropouts.*

Source: Alliance for Excellent Education, 2006

According to a 2008 Pew Center of States Study, there were a total of 2,319,258 adults held in American prisons or jails at the beginning of 2008. This amounts to more than 1% of our adult population or one for every 99.1 adults in America. Within that population, men are 13 times more likely to be incarcerated than women. In addition, black males make up the largest percentage of the prison population, with one in every nine black men in America between the ages of 20 to 34 behind bars. In 2007, the U.S. Census Bureau reported that there are more than three times as many black men living in prison cells than in college dormitories. This should spur any educator, or human being for that matter, on to action at the thought of the Titanic-like journey that awaits a newborn black baby boy the moment he is born.

The cost of managing our country's prison population, which happens to be the largest in the world, is astronomical. States spent more than $49 billion on prison in 2008, a massive $11 billion more than was spent in 1988. While the costs vary from state to state, this makes for an expense of nearly $58 a day per inmate. Such a cost has become so burdensome on states that drastic measures are being taken to prevent overcrowding facilities that are often millions over budget. In 2009, federal judges in California ordered that the state begin to make plans to release some 57,000 prisoners, more than one third of the state's prison population, back into society over a three-year period (Henderson, 2009). Shortsighted measures like these may reduce the cost of running prison facilities, but they do nothing to reduce crime and keep our citizens safe. The best answer is a long-term approach to promoting higher education at a young age.

Studies conducted in 2004 indicated that a simple 5% increase in the number of male high school graduates would lead to an annual crime-related savings of more than $5 billion (Alliance for Excellent Education, 2006). In addition, an additional $2.8 billion in earnings from productive adults would enter the economy. Such earnings would dramatically increase if these same adults went on to earn college degrees, while at the same time making our society safer and breaking generational cycles of crime that exist within impoverished areas of our communities.

Unemployment, poverty, and crime make for a triple threat to societal wealth in America. While all pose separate but equally challenging problems, the tie that binds them is education. Or, more accurately, a lack thereof. Through this data, we find that the level to which a person is educated either drastically increases or decreases their financial, physical, and emotional wellness. Whether you agree or disagree, accept or dispute this information, is up to you. However, to deny the fact that millions of American families are struggling unnecessarily because of a lack of education is like an ostrich poking its head into the sand. This struggle has become pervasive throughout our society and generational among families.

Our acceptance of such a reality is the first step that enables us to move from knowing to doing. It's time for educators to make decisions shaped around this data. It's time to leave procrastination to the status quo and develop meaningful, results-oriented changes in our classrooms that affect student learning today. It's time to elevate our professionalism and embrace our share of responsibility for the academic achievement of all students, no matter their circumstances. It's time to spread our passion to our colleagues for what is the noblest profession on earth, and to do so in the same manner with which we did when we first became educators. It's time for action.

THEORY TO PRACTICE

ITEMS FOR ARTICULATION

❏ Of the statistics referenced, which ones cause you to be concerned and/or take action?

❏ How might you use this data with your colleagues in order to promote change?

ITEMS FOR ACTION

❏ With your team, translate this data into kid-friendly terms in order to generate a better understanding of the value of a college education. Do the same for parents. Some examples of this might be to:

1. Create a game show in classrooms or during an assembly to bring these statistics to life.

2. Develop a PowerPoint that includes these statistics alongside inspirational stories about famous college graduates.

3. Create posters to place around the school displaying data about the value of a college education as well as information related to what it takes to enter a certain profession.

KEY CONCEPTS

"I will take a verb over a noun any day."

— William P. Young

1 The dynamic change that is taking place within successful No Excuses Universities is happening not because of theory, but because of practice.

2 There is no such thing as "college readiness" at the high-school level; that's called "college prep."

3 College readiness is the belief that all students should be taught in a way that prepares them for college if they choose to attend.

4 Talk is not cheap; it's actually very expensive. Because of this, it is crucial that schools operate with an action-oriented attitude towards continuous improvement.

TIME FOR ACTION

I don't know about you, but there have been times when I have noticed that my walk was not in sync with my talk. In fact, there were even periods where my beliefs about what was important professionally were distant from my ability to practically apply those truths to my work in the classroom or the principal's office. When personal reflection was not enough to align these two paths, I always made it a point to seek the support of others. Sometimes friends and colleagues would spotlight these shortcomings to me in an effort to help re-calibrate my inner professional compass. But on other occasions, I found clarity simply by observing the wisdom of those with far greater experience than my own.

On a chilly December evening in 1995, the Malden Mills textile factory tragically burnt to the ground. This company, specializing in the production of Polartec© fleece, was one of the largest employers in the relatively small community of Lawrence, Massachusetts. Owned and operated since the time of its inception by Aaron Feuerstein and his family, Malden Mills and the lives of its 3,000 employees were turned upside down overnight. Within days, every worker was summoned to a company meeting assumed to be a mere formality before the announcement of layoff notices. Packed into an auditorium, the employees burst into tears as Mr. Feuerstein shared his unexpected plan for the company. Rather than collect the more than $300 million in insurance money, Mr. Feuerstein decided to invest every penny to rebuild the factory. As if that were not enough, this modern-day hero paid the salaries of every employee for months as the mill was reconstructed. When asked why he chose to spend the money rather than retire a very wealthy man, Aaron Feuerstein laughed and said, "And what would I do? Eat more? Buy another suit? Retire and die? No, that was never an option" (60 Minutes, Safer, 2002). He didn't base his decision on money, he said. "I did it because it was the right thing to do."

The idea of knowing what is right, the *theory*, is very different from doing what is right, the *practice*. Just as Aaron Feuerstein modeled to his employees servant leadership that was grounded in action, today's educators must also act with similar behavior on behalf of their students. *To understand the difference between the theoretical and the practical is not enough.* Our students will only realize their greatest potential when we are focused on the *action* associated with turning theory into practice.

There's no doubt that the data referenced thus far are incredibly compelling to anyone with a passion for promoting change in the lives of students. However, it's still just data. It's just numbers. As Homer Simpson once said, "Oh, people can come up with statistics to prove anything. Fourteen percent of people know that." Surprisingly, Homer's cartoonish remark has some validity to the discussion that is taking place between you as the reader and me as the author. These statistics were not written on paper so that they could be stored up for the reader to recall during conversations at happy hour or as answers to random trivia dialogues during morning commutes. The purpose of this data is to spur on action. It's a simple concept, but one that escapes thousands upon thousands of educators who participate in professional development workshops or yearly book clubs. (If you are reading this as part of your yearly book club, then forgive my last comment.) The dynamic change that is taking place within successful No Excuses Universities is happening not because of theory but instead because of practice.

Albert Einstein once said, "The world is a dangerous place, not because of those who do evil, but because of those who look on and do nothing." Such is true when it comes to our world of education. We are living in a monumental time in which educators have greater access than ever to strategies and ideas that are proven to make a difference in the educational and social lives of students. Research proves many of these ideas and yet we seem to be stagnant as an industry. Public education in particular has become the finest scapegoat that exists when one wishes to cast blame for society's ills. Truth be told, in many ways it's been our own fault. But unlike those who seek to throw stones at enormous issues such as a lack of funding, massive educational bureaucracies, labor unions, etc., I believe the problem is far less complicated. Our problem is that we wait too long to act.

At the beginning of Los Pen's college-readiness initiative, we found no examples of similar work taking place at the elementary school level. In fact, we were told by many both inside our district and beyond that "college readiness is a high school matter." Some of our nation's largest college-support endeavors only begin promoting college readiness at the junior high school level. This in my opinion is not a knock against the fine work that is taking place within those organizations, but more so a representation of a lack of initiative on the parts of elementary school educators. For years, elementary educators have allowed a top-down approach in regard to meaningful school reform. While high schools and junior high schools introduce students to an increasingly rigorous curriculum, elementary staff members have been seen by many as the "nurturers" whose first job is to teach students the "love of learning." What a crock! Most elementary school teachers would agree that this depiction of K-6 work could not be further from reality. In fact, most educators from all levels recognize that one of the hardest things to do within our field is to teach a five, six, or seven-year-old how to read. Unfortunately, as confident as we are in the importance of our role, we act with a meekness that marginalizes our credibility and stifles our influence. Knowing this, how must educators, especially those at the elementary level, take their place at the table of reform in order to create massive change? The answer quite simply is to *act*.

Elementary educators must never underestimate the power that they have in changing the life of a child. Furthermore, they must never assume that it is too early to begin making that change. But change cannot take place without the action of a practitioner. Sure, in our hearts and even in our words we profess the belief in our ability to change lives, especially when speaking to parents or community members. But how many times have you known someone to act contrary to this belief on your own campus? Go ahead; think of the name of a teacher, administrator, or classified employee at your school that "talks the talk" in public, but lacks the deeds that reinforce such a belief within the classroom. Talk without action and theory without practice is a killer for change and hence impedes the progress that is so desperately required to offer hope to a student in need. When we look at the data and are convinced that our cause is just (and it is), and we believe that our purpose is clear (and it is), then our job is to move forward with a tenacious spirit that is reflective of the importance of our mission. That mission, which is one that is all-encompassing to both transforming a school's culture and a student's life, is that of college readiness. Whether you are a kindergarten teacher in the inner city of Los Angeles or an eighth-grade mathematics instructor in a suburb outside of Chicago, it's time to take your seat at the table. If you agree that education is the best way to a successful life, and for our most at-risk students is the only realistic means to escape the grip of poverty, then it's time for action. The first course for action is that of deciding upon a clear understanding and definition of the term *college readiness*.

What is College Readiness?

If we can trace the root of our downfall, which is seen so clearly in the data provided thus far, why is it that we continue to have an abundance of public schools failing in our country? Many would lead you to believe that the answer to this question is so complex that it would take decades for Ivy League scholars to determine. It is my contention, however, that the answer comes down to a lack of focus from the time children step foot as kindergarteners, and sometimes even earlier, in our schools.

Everywhere you go, you will find a plethora of schools that are thematic in nature. Many schools are "tech" schools that focus their attention on exposing their students to the latest technology that exists. Other schools plant their flag on the subject of writing, making sure that everything done in the school has some kind of a writing focus. Still others align themselves directly with a series of programs with the hope that mandated unity will create long-term literacy results for their students. While these schools have their fair share of benefits and oftentimes find ways to produce immediate academic results for students, they fail to reinforce what I believe to be the most important long-term theme needed by children today, that of college readiness.

In my work with schools across the country, I spend much of my time battling a misperception held by some of our most talented educators. From teachers, to principals, to superintendents and other high-ranking district officials, I continually hear talk about the importance of promoting college readiness in high school. This discussion, and the numerous goals presented around this idea, is as fundamentally flawed as anything that exists today in public education. The idea that college readiness begins in high school is as senseless as the idea that parenting begins when children become teenagers. In fact, I would suggest that there is no such thing as "college readiness" at high school; rather, there is only "college prep." To the outside observer, these may appear to be synonymous; however, I assure you that they are both quite different.

College prep concepts can be found in many schools, typically beginning in sixth grade and moving up through high school. Schools offer college prep classes in an effort to expose students to more challenging courses that present an academic rigor parallel to that which they may find at the university level. And while this concept is an excellent one for students who are determined to pursue a college degree someday, they do nothing for students who may lack the fundamental understanding of the benefits of higher education. In addition, because participation in these courses is often an expectation of those living in upper- to middle-class households, students of poverty are all too often left out of the mix because they don't receive the same encouragement to enroll in such classes from their parents. Because of this, they are solely dependent on what we as educators promote to them in our individual schools. Though many educators would dispute the fact, our track record on endorsing the possibility of college for every child is one that is not supported by the data mentioned thus far. Let's take a look at a typical scenario.

Arturo and his family moved to the United States from Mexico when he was four years old. Immediately he was enrolled in school, where he began to learn English at an early age. Over time his skills in reading and math became average as he left elementary school and attended junior high. Arturo's parents were proud of his progress and found themselves dependent on his grasp of the English language as they themselves had failed to learn how to read, write, or speak English with any kind of fluency. As he entered high school, Arturo had become the only member of his family to be educated beyond the eighth grade. In sitting down with his school counselor, he was presented with two options. The first was to participate in college prep classes that would not only expose him to a challenging curriculum, but also bring the possibility in some cases of earning college credit. The second option was to participate in the high school diploma track that would prove successful as long as he received a "D" or better in every course. Arturo thought about the challenge of the college prep courses and understood that while his grades were average, these courses sounded just too challenging. In addition, he believed that college was a place where "rich kids" went and because he lived in very humble circumstances, he thought his chances to be slim. It didn't take long for Arturo to decide on the diploma track. After four years, with great praise from his teaches and incredible pride on the part of his parents, Arturo graduated from high school. He soon found that the diploma he had earned was not exactly a key to long-term financial stability. Over the years, he worked several different jobs in order to make ends meet. Before he knew it, Arturo had a family of his own. In spite of his hard work in high school and the diploma that he proudly hung in a frame on his wall, the cycle was about to continue all over again with his own children.

Stories like these are all too common when we operate with a flawed understanding and belief that college prep is actually college readiness. College readiness begins the moment students step foot in elementary school. No Excuses Universities live by the true definition of college readiness:

"College readiness is not the idea that every student will go to college. It is the idea that every student deserves the opportunity to be prepared to enroll in college if they so choose to attend. Furthermore, beginning in elementary school, it is the responsibility of educators to make this

concept come to life for each student regardless of their academic or social background."

With this definition, it's now time to learn the details that will help you create a college readiness revolution of your own. As you read, you will discover practical strategies and ideas that can be implemented immediately at your school site or throughout your district. I urge you to go forward with an action-oriented passion that seeks not to make changes for students one, two, or three years from now, but for the children in your classrooms today. As Super Bowl champion coach Steve Mariucci once said, "I don't even wear a watch; the time is always now." With that spirit, let's get started.

THEORY TO PRACTICE

ITEMS FOR ARTICULATION

❏ How effective are your team and staff meetings? Do the conversations that take place at these meetings spur individuals on to action?

❏ Think of the behaviors that make for a productive or unproductive meeting. Which behaviors should be reinforced to create success? Which behaviors should be reduced to stifle negativity?

ITEMS FOR ACTION

❏ As a school, find consensus to create your definition of the term "college readiness." After doing so, display this definition in prominent areas of the school in order to ensure understanding by all stakeholders.

KEY CONCEPTS

"People often say that motivation doesn't last. Well, neither does bathing—that's why we recommend it daily."

— Zig Ziglar

1 "Powerful symbolism" is used to market a college readiness message through flags, signage, spirit wear, and school-wide incentive programs.

2 When done right, marketing can make a school's purpose come to life.

3 Individual classrooms select different universities to partner with in an effort to expose students to the concept of college.

4 Powerful symbolism helps to unite students, families, and staff members.

MARKETING THE MESSAGE

S ometimes the mother of invention communicates in very unconventional ways. For Bill Bowerman, that could not have been more true. In the early 1970s, this very successful University of Oregon track coach was in search of innovative methods to make his athletes faster. One day while working in his garage, he concocted a liquid urethane solution and poured it into his wife's waffle iron. What resulted was an interlocking square pattern that was perfect for the bottom of an athletic shoe. This creative idea that began in one man's workshop has become the most recognizable athletic shoe and apparel company in the world. Named for the Greek goddess of victory, Nike is one of America's greatest success stories. Its swoosh has become as recognizable as the McDonald's golden arches and Disneyland's Mickey Mouse. As equally impressive as the genesis of Nike is the way in which this company markets its message.

From the moment Nike employees fill out their W-2s, they begin to learn about the history of the organization. Described as "internal branding" by *Fast Company Magazine* in 2007, the Nike Storytelling Program teaches all new hires the importance of knowing their roots as well as the value of consistently living by their mission. What others see simply as a little white "swoosh" Nike employees see as an icon that was once sold out of the back of a car by co-founder Phil Knight. The words "Just Do It" may act as an unforgettable catch phrase that prompts you and me to exercise more, but to the 30,000-plus members of Nike, it represents a call to outside-the-box thinking. While Nike understands the importance of spending millions on marketing their product to those outside their headquarters, they know that such spending becomes futile if they do not take the time to cultivate believers within.

The same holds true for today's schools. Many administrators are constantly in search of the right school reform book that will change the culture and solve the ills that have existed within their schools for years. As an author of such a book, I certainly would not knock the value of this act. However, I would offer a step that must be accomplished in tandem—that is to also observe the lessons learned from those in the world of marketing. It has been my experience that the latter is rarely pursued. Unfortunately, this has resulted in short-lived success for many very good school initiatives. This was a lesson learned early on by my staff and me as we created the No Excuses University.

Why is Marketing So Important?

The Super Bowl is played every year in order to crown the champion team of the NFL. The games are often exciting, as some of the world's best athletes display physical talents admired by many. All this and what do we watch? The commercials. In 2008, the Fox Network reportedly received $2.7 million for each 30-second commercial aired during the Super Bowl. This astonishing figure pales in comparison to the yearly amount spent on marketing food to children. In 2008, the Federal Trade Commission reported that $1.6 billion was spent on marketing food and drinks to children 17 and under. Whether a one-day event or a consistent yearly plan, marketing like this has resulted in millions attending movies, buying cereal, or purchasing electronics that collectively generate trillions in profits for U.S. companies. The lesson: marketing works!

From car companies that sell a new brand of SUV, to a principal who sells an idea to his staff, the premise of marketing is the same. When done right, marketing primarily does two things. First, it inspires people. For a company, it inspires consumers to spend money. For a school, it inspires educators to act differently. Second, marketing creates a symbolism that stands for something and prompts a specific thought. As we see with Nike, their powerful swoosh makes us think of sports or maybe exercise. For students who attend a No Excuses University, our logo reminds them that their paramount goal is to graduate from college. Many would argue that marketing is simply a form of brainwashing. While there may be some truth in this, I would suggest that marketing is more about the power to persuade people. Granted, it can certainly be used to encourage individuals to make poor decisions. However, it can also be used for good. The work of promoting college readiness to students is, at its core, noble. When you blend this nobility with a commitment to market a college readiness message in schools, you get what we refer to as *powerful symbolism*.

WHAT IS POWERFUL SYMBOLISM?

Powerful symbolism is the visible marketing of a school's number one goal. In short, it makes a school's purpose come to life. While this symbolism may express many ideas, such as character traits or academic expectations, the message that ties them all together is the same. For some schools, that message may be the exposure to the arts or a thematic focus on literacy. However, we find that the best, all-encompassing purpose is that of promoting college readiness to all students. The beauty of this focus is that so much of this work, and the powerful symbolism ideas that go with it, are able to fall under the college readiness umbrella.

Powerful symbolism unites teachers, excites parents, and motivates students. It can be implemented on any campus across the country no matter the demographics of a school or budgetary status of a district. Unlike other reform efforts, the implementation of powerful symbolism can be affordable and swift. As you read of the many ways that No Excuses Universities expose their students to powerful symbolism, ask yourself, "How can we modify these ideas to meet the needs of our school's purpose?" If your purpose is in line with a mission to promote college readiness for all, don't hesitate to take advantage of the ideas listed throughout the remainder of this chapter. (Find out more about how your school can officially join the No Excuses University Network of Schools in chapter 13.) With that in mind, take a look at all of the ways that you can begin promoting powerful symbolism right away.

University Adoptions: One of the first steps that schools must take in creating a college readiness culture is to have every classroom adopt a different university. The process of selecting universities can be done in a variety of ways but in the end should ensure a wide exposure to many universities and colleges across the coun- try. No school should have two classrooms that represent the same university, as the idea is to present as many options to students as possible. Schools are encouraged to garner the participation of the office staff, librarian, custodian, and all specialists to join in this

process as well. Each staff member should select a university they would like to represent. Once every staff member has done so, college flags or banners should be hung outside their door. This visual message conveys a powerful statement about your school's purpose and excites students, parents, and staff. This excitement, blended with the creation of the six exceptional systems described at the beginning of the book, have the potential to produce sustainable positive academic and social success for all students.

The process of selecting universities is one that has stimulated many questions from the thousands of educators with whom I have had the pleasure to work. In fact, it has been the most popular subject line on the emails I've received over the last several years. Because of this, I have listed some FAQs in the hope that I can clarify questions that you may have when it comes to adopting different universities.

Are selections based on whether or not a teacher or staff member is an alumnus of a particular university?

No. We have found that a high percentage of schools have educators who have received degrees from the same university. Had Los Pen used this as a rule for teachers, San Diego State University flags would be hanging on the outside of about half of our doors. But because of the spirit that is associated with being a graduate from a specific university, we always let alumni choose their own schools whenever possible.

What do you do if two people want to select the same university?

Flip a coin or play rock-paper-scissors. Yes, I'm serious. I have heard stories of teachers getting into arguments over the selection of a university. This completely defeats the purpose. Make your selections and then move on to the important work of promoting college readiness for all.

Should we select community colleges and trade schools?

The view of No Excuses Universities is that elementary schools should focus on promoting four-year universities, middle and junior high schools should add community colleges into the mix, and high schools should blend in the possibility of trade schools as part of their support of students. To suggest to five- or six-year-olds that they should think about community college or trade school as an option is not only playing the role of fortuneteller—it makes unfair suggestions about their abilities to succeed at the same level as many of their peers. As you will read in future chapters, this plan for promoting college readiness is not a knock against community colleges or trade schools but instead grounded purely on data.

Must a university adopt your class before you can adopt them?

After staff members select a university to represent, the goal is to get that same university to adopt their classroom back. That said, it is not a prerequisite for choosing your university. What makes for a great partnership between a class and a university? Find out in chapter 11.

Classroom Bulletin Boards: One of the greatest experiences for students is the creation of a college bulletin board within their classroom. Classroom teachers work with their students to find facts about their particular university that spark interest and act as fuel for continuous conversation. The best boards are those that are always changing throughout the year as a result of new information found by

students, parents, and teachers or sent to the classroom by representatives of the university.

College-Bound Bulletin Boards: Many schools have found that motivating students about college is as easy as a map, a few pictures, pushpins, and some string. The process could not be simpler. Gather individual pictures from every staff member who has earned a college degree. Post them on a centrally located bulletin board in the hallway, office, or

school entrance with lots of foot traffic. Place a U.S. map in the center of the board and have teachers connect a string from their pictures to the locations of the universities from which they earned their degrees. You will be amazed at how many conversations take place in front of boards like these.

Monday Spirit Wear: Most schools offer spirit wear with the school slogan or logo printed on the front or back for students to purchase. When it comes to the promotion of college readiness, however, there are three simple changes that can be made in order to create powerful symbolism. First, create t-shirts with a college readiness focus that markets your message. Second, ask all students, staff, and parents to wear their shirts every Monday in an effort to set the stage for the week ahead. Finally, ensure that every student receives a shirt no matter his or her socioeconomic background. The value of having all students display powerful symbolism and wear their shirts on the same day far outweighs the cost of purchasing t-shirts for those who cannot afford to do so on their own.

(Please note that only schools that have officially been accepted into the No Excuses University™ Network of Schools and received written consent are allowed to use the trademarked No Excuses University name and logo. Find out more in chapter 13.)

Friday University Gear: End your week by encouraging students to wear the apparel supporting the university that their classroom has adopted. Some classrooms that have been adopted back by their university may be fortunate enough to have shirts donated to them, while other classes may have students make their own spirit wear as part of an art project. Still others may simply ask students to wear the school colors. Wearing university apparel every Friday is another display of powerful college symbolism that sends a school community into the weekend with high spirits.

Character Traits: The promotion of college readiness must be done in such a way that not only focuses on the academic skills necessary for a student to be successful, but also the social skills needed to make wise decisions as well. Focusing on specific character traits helps to do just that. The key is to have schools choose traits that are wide-reaching and comprehensive in nature. With so many traits to choose from, some schools get carried away, selecting a dozen or more. In the end, the quantity produces little quality in learning; students become overwhelmed with too

many traits. Along with many of the schools within the No Excuses University Network, I have found the Character Counts program to be exceptional. This program, founded by Michael Josephson, focuses on six traits that are broad enough to include every major value that one can think of, but specific enough to act as a springboard for meaningful conversations between students and staff. Learn more about this terrific program by visiting www. charactercounts.org.

Murals: Experience shows us that hallways and playgrounds are the most likely locations for behavior problems with students. Because of this, many schools have spent time, and in some cases money, to paint murals

in strategic locations that remind students of the high academic and social expectations that we have of them. If your school does not have the resources or time to make this happen right away, do what many schools have done by making this a yearly promotion gift to the school from fifth, sixth, or eighth graders. This value-added philosophy will create a substantial amount of powerful symbolism in just a few short years.

Signage: As a successful Title I school, Los Peñasquitos Elementary receives hundreds of visitors a year from all over the country. Over and over, people describe how they "felt differently" the moment they stepped foot on our campus. This is thanks in large part to the signage that is displayed at every turn. When visitors drive up to the school, they notice our large No Excuses University logo. Upon walking through the office, they read the Los Pen Pledge, which is painted on the wall: "We are committed to creating a school that knows no limits to the academic success of each student." When

they look up, they see carefully selected slogans that promote our belief in students and their ability to attend college. Don't get me wrong; I'm not suggesting that you make your school walls look like buildings in Time Square, but I do believe that strategically placed signage can stimulate the physical environment of any school.

Mascot Books: In 2003, Naren and Aimee Aryal founded Mascot Books Publishing. This company creates and publishes books that tell the story of universities through the eyes of their mascot. To an elementary school librarian, this is a godsend. It provides exciting literature that is aligned with a school's college readiness purpose. Just as many librarians have experienced, you will find that these books

are tough to keep on the shelves. Visit www.mascotbooks. com for more information.

College-Themed Incentive Programs: Having an all-encompassing theme like college readiness makes it very easy for schools to shift their powerful symbolism focus without having to do away with the successful programs that already exist on site.

For example, there are many schools that participate in reading incentive programs. Los Pen used to organize a yearly program titled "Reading Olympics" in which students were encouraged to read a certain amount of books in order to earn a gold, silver, or bronze metal. Upon the creation of the No Excuses University, we changed the name of this program to "Read Your Way to College" and instead awarded students bachelor's, master's, and Ph.D. awards. While we changed the name and the awards, we didn't change the focus of the program. Examples like these can be found in the numerous programs that exist in our schools today. Whether you make a change from "Olympic Field Day" to "College Field Day," or replace a field trip to a museum with a field trip to a college campus, the theme of college readiness is easily incorporated.

The success of No Excuses University has led many educators who participate in this endeavor to offer opinions for what makes this model so special. Ed Rafferty, superintendent of District 54 in Schaumburg, Illinois, said, "No Excuses acts as the hook that gets all stakeholders excited about learning and motivates them to find new and better ways to get results." This description is especially appropriate when it comes to the creation of powerful symbolism on a campus. The marketing of a college readiness theme is a vital part of the inspiration that is needed at every school that wishes to shift the mindset of a student body. Schools that have marketed these ideas are not only implementing them with ease; they are also finding new and innovative ways to promote powerful symbolism unique to their own sites. The strategies offered thus far are practical and simple to follow, leaving little excuse for anyone to sit idle on the sidelines.

THEORY TO PRACTICE

ITEMS FOR ARTICULATION

❏ This chapter provides numerous examples of powerful symbolism that can exist on a school campus. Which ideas could be implemented tomorrow? Which ones might take more time?

❏ How is your school currently displaying powerful symbolism? How might you make adjustments so that your school reflects a spirit of college readiness?

ITEMS FOR ACTION

❏ As a school, create a "powerful symbolism" committee with members from each grade level. The job of this committee is to:

1. Gather inspirational quotations and mottos to display on signs throughout the school.

2. Work with grade-level teams to select individual universities for each classroom.

3. Design a college readiness t-shirt for every student to wear each Monday.

4. Work with your PTA, foundation, community supporters, and district to generate the funds necessary to purchase powerful symbolism items.

Decide upon a timeline for implementing each step mentioned above. Most schools set a target of two to three months to have all of their powerful symbolism in place.

KEY CONCEPTS

ℚ

"Ninety-nine percent of the failures come from people who have the habit of making excuses."

— George Washington

1 Those who wait for everyone to "get on board" will be waiting forever.

2 Failure to achieve results is never an indictment of the naysayers; it's an indictment of the *closet optimists* who lack the will to take a stand.

3 The promotion of college readiness must be more than window dressing. It has to be grounded in collaborative work that takes place behind the scenes.

4 Every adult on campus has a duty to model appropriate behavior and character in a unified way.

No Excuses Begins with the Staff

S an Jacinto Elementary School is located in an impoverished area of Amarillo, Texas where more than 95% of the students are considered economically disadvantaged. Every year, one third of the students, who live primarily in the low-income rental properties adjacent to the school, move outside the San Jacinto attendance area as new families move in. For years, this steady mobility rate came with a consistent level of academic student achievement that matched the basic expectations of most schools on a lower socioeconomic level. Test scores in all subjects were either near or at the bottom compared to other schools within the Amarillo School District. But the silver lining in the existence of San Jacinto Elementary had always been the school's tendency to employ warmhearted teachers who cared for children and were professional with each other. Still, in spite of the efforts of this collegial staff, the learning that took place was never enough to provide any kind of hope for children who were in desperate need of escaping a life of poverty.

In the eyes of many, San Jacinto was doing as well as could be expected. The community, while supportive as a whole, still focused primarily on the basic needs of students and families: food, clothing, school supplies, etc. A pervasive attitude existed both inside and outside of San Jacinto: "these students" simply had too many problems to even care about learning. There were, at times, pockets of excellence, but these successes were never sustainable from one classroom or grade level to the next. In 2005, state assessments revealed that 70% of the students were proficient in reading, 78% in writing, 60% in math, and 40% in science. While much better than many of the scores earned by similar schools, these marks still kept San Jacinto in danger of being labeled an "academically unacceptable" campus by the state of Texas.

Fed up with the status quo, Principal Doug Curry and three teachers from his school attended a TurnAround Schools Institute about the No Excuses University model. As the San Jacinto staff members heard about the steps necessary to create a *Culture of Universal Achievement*, develop *exceptional systems*, and foster a learning environment focused on promoting college readiness for all, one teacher turned to another and said, "We would have been elated if our kids simply made it through high school."

Principal Curry, along with his teachers, left the conference with a clear understanding that the expectations for their students were much too low. With a newfound excitement for teaching and a courageous spirit to influence their colleagues, these staff members presented the lessons learned from the conference, hoping that a rebirth would take place on the San Jacinto campus. Their passion captivated the rest of the staff and created a movement that day that surprised everyone. After brief discussions among teachers during their lunch break, every single staff member proclaimed their desire to adopt the tenets of the No Excuses University model. Amazed by the immediate positive feedback, Principal Curry challenged the staff to consider the possible ridicule that would come from others when a school known for poor academic results suddenly declared itself to be a new kind of "college preparatory" school. The staff's fearless response was simple: "Bring it on!"

Since that moment, San Jacinto has undergone a transformation that rivals that of any similar school in the country. In one year, student academic results skyrocketed: 92% proficiency in reading, 92% in writing, 95% in math, and 90% in science. For the first time in the history of San Jacinto, the school achieved "recognized" status by the state of Texas.

The transformation was so great that the community of Amarillo not only noticed but rushed to provide support.

San Jacinto Elementary was asked to participate in the ACE program (Achievement through Commitment to Education). Funded by local philanthropists, ACE ensures that students who maintain a certain grade point average, attendance in school, and level of acceptable behavior will have their entire college tuition paid for if they choose to attend the local two-year community college (Amarillo College) and local university (West Texas A&M). So inspired by the change that has taken place at San Jacinto, Amarillo College has forged a unique adoption by offering college courses and GED opportunities on the elementary campus as a service to San Jacinto parents.

The San Jacinto Elementary story continues to inspire educators working at schools that face similar challenges. The transformation that began in 2007 has been a sustaining one. The school earned the highest status of success in the state of Texas, "exemplary," in 2009. While San Jacinto is still in its infancy as a No Excuses University, the staff, students, and parents are more committed than ever to making the dream of college become a reality.

Is Everyone on Board?

The San Jacinto Elementary example is reflective of stories that are common throughout the No Excuses University network of schools. Like most NEU schools, the staff at San Jacinto recognized their need to embrace their reality, challenge their results, and ask, "Can we provide a better education for our students than the one we are currently giving them?" The answer may not have been abundantly clear the moment they began their journey, but it certainly is today. The results earned by the San Jacinto staff were not a product of casting blame or even dwelling on the past. The results came from their humble act of acceptance and willingness to change.

In my work with schools, I've seen my share of educators who swear that they are up against insurmountable odds. Some insist that their job duties are too large and their paycheck is too small, yet the funny thing is ... they keep showing up to work! The reality is that they will continue to show up every day, with no plans to change. Educators like these place a tremendous responsibility on students and parents and demand a level of excellence from others that they don't from themselves. Do you see the hypocrisy in their attitude? What a waste of time for them personally. What a tragedy for kids. In the midst of their complaints, many of these same individuals talk about their desire to be a part of something special but suggest that they are dependent on others to make that happen. At best we can chalk up their view of such school transformation as *skewed*; at worst it can be seen as *blatant excuse-making*. Through my research and personal experiences, I have found that not a single school turned around until **individuals** made the decision to cast aside their beliefs of *what should be* and focus on what is. I have shared with thousands of educators: It's all right to be jaded by politicians and bureaucracy, but never at the cost of becoming apathetic about the potential of a student. The best defense of such apathy is to maintain an outlook that is open to change.

As we know, change is never easy, especially in the world of education. In fact, change may be the single biggest cause of fear for those within our profession. Whether certificated or classified, employees not only fear change; they fight it. You and I could name a dozen adults with whom we have worked who have made a career out of fighting change. Many have become so sidetracked by this fight that teaching becomes secondary. In the end, some of our most needy students are left out in the cold as the perpetual cycle of poor instruction continues from one year to the next. As shameful as this small group of educators is, there is actually a group that I find more disappointing. I refer to them as the *closet optimists*.

Several years ago, I began working with a school just outside Seattle, Washington. Located in a small rural community, this elementary school experienced results that depleted the morale among staff as it entered into program improvement status. Wanting to learn more about their challenges, I studied the results of a recent survey taken by the staff. This survey, which consisted of just two simple questions, told me everything that I needed to know about the school. When asked "Do you believe that all students can learn?" 90% of the staff answered, "Yes." When given question number two, "Do you believe that all of your colleagues believe that all students can learn?" 90% answered, "No." The analysis was simple. Ninety percent of this staff believed that they were among the minority of believers with the view that all students could learn. It was amazing! So much so, that I decided to candidly—and bluntly—share the results with them. My conversation went something like this:

"Today, I have great news for 90% of you, and very bad news for 10% of you. First, the good news: Ninety percent of you believe in the potential of your students. That is incredible and it is something that we are going to capitalize on. Now for the bad news: Ninety percent of you think that you are alone in this belief. I am guessing that this is because 10% of this staff does all the talking, voices all the viewpoints, and somehow believes that they represent the opinions of this staff. If that is the case and you are in that 10%, here is my message to you ... shut up. If on the other hand, however, you are in the critical mass of the 90% who does believe in the potential of all students and their innate ability to learn, then my message is one that is even stronger to you ... speak up! To allow the naysayers on this campus to voice a negative opinion about the students of this school while at the same time marginalizing the positive influence that the critical mass of you hold, is not an indictment on the negativity of the 10%. It is an indictment on the meekness of the 90%."

You could have heard a pin drop. As the faces of two or three teachers began to show frustration, the faces of twenty

111

others began to break out with a smile. They had been liberated while being called to action at the same time.

The critical mass of this small school in Washington had been behaving like closet optimists. A closet optimist is someone who is very positive and driven on the inside, but incredibly quiet and submissive on the outside. They are the people who might share how badly they would like to take part in innovative practices, but only if "everyone is on board." The reality for a closet optimist is that he or she will end up waiting forever, because there is no such thing as a staff where everyone is on board. The reason for this is simple: The negativity of most naysayers stems not from their educational philosophy, but from personal issues that may haunt them outside of the school. Think about it for a minute. Have you ever met a teacher who was negative and rude within his or her classroom or on campus, but who, the moment he or she left the gates of the school, became hospitable and encouraging as a person? It doesn't happen! The reason why people do not get on board at school is because they are generally not on board in life. And as sad as this is for them as individuals, what is worse is when an entire staff becomes hostage to such behavior. If the critical mass of a staff is hesitant to charge forward with a "no excuses" attitude until everyone is on board, results will remain status quo at best and student learning will suffer. And because No Excuses begins with the staff, this is a battle that must be decisively won at the beginning of a school's transformation process.

More than Window Dressing

As displayed by the previous examples encouraging the creation of powerful symbolism, the visible steps necessary to create a spirit of college readiness are fairly straightforward and simple. The power of a college readiness message that has been strategically marketed to students, parents, and staff is truly inspirational. However, if not accompanied by concrete steps taken behind the scenes, this inspiration will be short lived and educators may be left asking themselves, "Where are the results?" As described by numerous NEU educators across the nation, the real work of our college readiness endeavor is not found in what is seen, but rather in what is unseen. As a school begins the process of hanging flags outside of doors and in hallways, staff members must assume the responsibility of bringing the concept of college to life within the classroom in ways that may not be immediately visible to typical passerby. To assist your progress through your own college readiness journey, I have outlined a step-by-step plan that will help move your school beyond the window dressing. I would suggest that these steps be completed along with your school's implementation of college readiness symbolism. Remember that all of your efforts must consistently dovetail with the work that every school should undertake in the development of the TurnAround Schools model of six exceptional systems. These systems, displayed briefly in chapter two of this book and in great detail in the book *TurnAround Schools: Creating Cultures of Universal Achievement*, must always guide your endeavor.

Step One: Define a unified language that promotes the concept of college.

While every school is unique, the idea of instilling a unified language that promotes college does not have to be. Depending on their levels (elementary, middle, high, etc.), schools should unify and create a list of words that are infused in the daily conversations between teachers, students, and parents. From the word "college" that is taught to kindergarteners to the words "major" and "dissertation" that might be taught to fourth, fifth, or sixth-graders, students should be offered a college-going language from their teachers the same way my kids learned their ABCs from Elmo on Sesame Street. It doesn't have to be difficult, nor should it become a point for contention or debate by staff members. Each grade level should decide upon a list of five to ten words to reinforce on a daily basis. Much like the expansion of an adult's vocabulary over time, exposure to a unified language that promotes the concept of college should shift and grow from one year to the next.

Step Two: Seek ways to integrate the concept of college into existing subject matter.

My brother-in-law is a gifted photographer with a keen ability to find great pictures in situations that others do not. Most of his pictures are snapshots of our family, but he often has an urge to focus in on the minute details that nature provides. During these times, he shifts from a standard lens to a macro lens that highlights the features within a tropical

114

flower or a tiny hummingbird. A simple shift of his lens enables him to take pictures of activity unseen by the naked eye. I am always amazed at the product.

When it comes to promoting college readiness, our work within the classroom must be looked at through a different lens as well. Math problems that used to focus on calculating distances from one arbitrary place to another can be shifted to lessons that ask students to compute the driving distance between Duke University and Boston College. State history units that require students to write extensively about local landmarks can also expect them to focus on the history of the universities within their community. No matter the grade or subject, integrating the concept of college into the curriculum is easily done when viewed through a different lens. Every grade level or department should create a plan at the beginning of the year that weaves college readiness into the daily work of teaching and learning.

Step Three: Explicitly model college readiness behavior and expectations to students.

Explicit is an adjective that is defined as: *stated clearly in detail; leaving no room for confusion or doubt.* This word is used liberally but implemented much too rarely in our field. It's a shame, because the actions that accompany this powerful word have the potential to open doors for student learning. Rather than be straightforward in our teaching, we often assume that our students understand concepts that we are trying to explain. This is a huge mistake, especially when working with students of poverty. Schools within the No Excuses University network take the guesswork out of promoting college readiness as they explicitly describe the academic and social behaviors necessary to be successful in the present and the future. They explicitly model, practice, teach, and review these behaviors in a variety of ways on a regular basis. Each school takes the time to lay out a detailed plan for this process in an effort to unify the work of an entire staff. Some examples:

Unified Classroom Management Plan: Like most schools, each No Excuses University adopts a set of behavior expectations for students to observe. These expectations are centered on a limited number of character traits (no more than six) that coincide with the values displayed in a productive citizen. For us, the Character Counts blueprint of trustworthiness, respect, responsibility, fairness, caring, and citizenship offers structure for our plan to teach appropriate behavior. And I do mean teach.

Too often, educators focus on discipline rather than behavior modification. They act with the assumption that students should innately know right from wrong and therefore deserve punishment when they cross the line. I agree that there should always be consequences when rules are broken, but those consequences should never be doled out without an adult taking the time to reinforce appropriate behavior. When we fail to teach appropriate behavior, we are destined to find ourselves in the same exact situation with the same exact student in the future. Think about it for a moment. Does your school have lunch detention for your students? If it does, are the same students showing up in detention over and over again? The likely answer is yes. If that is the case, it is not because these students are innately bad; it is because the act of detention does not work for them. We discovered that this was exactly the case for many students at Los Pen. After years of lunch detention with the same students, we asked ourselves, "Is this working?" The data clearly showed that it was not. Therefore our mindset changed from being reactive to proactive. Instead of dealing with negative behavior after it took place, we decided to seek ways to stop it before poor decisions were made. From this thinking came a unified classroom management plan.

Every teacher implements and every staff member supports a behavior management plan that is universal from one classroom to the next. (This plan can be found in Appendix A.) All of our rules are based on the six character traits. When students break the rules after being given one warning, they take time to participate in "re-thinking" letters that force them to review the results of their actions. These letters are never used as busy work for a student, but rather are the catalyst for quality conversations between the teacher and the student. As negative behavior progresses, parents are brought into the mix and steps are taken immediately to set high expectations from the beginning of the year. Conversations with students during these times are candid and serious, but always respectful. We let students know how much we care about them, and that we are disappointed in their choices rather than in them. This lets the students know that they are capable of making different choices in the future. Because of such conversations, we have seen far fewer "frequent flyers," as we call them, to the office. In fact, our eyes have been opened by the positive effects that have come as a result of caring adults collectively embracing a school-wide behavior plan.

In addition to the consequences found within the unified management plan, we also focus on the numerous ways that a teacher can positively reinforce good behavior and character. This is crucial; we need to ensure that equal time is given to students who consistently exhibit appropriate behavior. These students are often overlooked and taken for granted. When our attention becomes consumed by the negative, many of our well-behaved students may veer off course in an effort to be noticed. Like all endeavors, no plan is perfect. There are certainly times where we reach the end of our rope in search of unique solutions for unique students. Still, we remain steadfast in our desire to find better ways to improve behavior. Any adult can discipline a student, but it takes a true teacher to help change behavior.

Exploration of College Entrance Standards: Along with the reinforcement of positive behavior, we also work to set lofty academic expectations. Each No Excuses University seeks to promote an understanding to students about what it takes to be prepared for college. Conversations about college entrance standards begin to take place in the upper grades as teachers break down a list of expectations that are required of students seeking entrance into public or private universities within a particular state. Some classrooms receive college application packets from their adopters and participate in mock enrollment lessons. Others take trips to university campuses and meet with guidance counselors or students as they learn about the choices that they can make today in order to influence their road to college tomorrow. From early on in elementary school until the moment students graduate from high school, teachers must invest time in providing clarity when it comes to expectations required of students who are college bound. A great book to help guide you in this journey is *College Knowledge* by David Conley.

College Readiness Celebration: In many of our poorer communities, there is a negative stigma attached with attending college. Often, this attitude is a defense mechanism for students who feel that the concept of college is an impossibility. And for students who come from generational poverty, who can blame them when all they have seen is one family member after another fail to make this idea a reality? The best means of changing their attitudes is to make the concept of college exciting and engaging. Students at many No Excuses Universities participate in weekly pep rallies, monthly awards ceremonies, and yearly college fairs. These events shun the attitudes of those who think that failing school is "no big deal" as they make excitement about learning the norm.

Step Four: Continuously collaborate in search of innovative and successful practices that strengthen your college readiness purpose.

The best gains ever achieved by No Excuses Universities have always come as a result of team members who work shoulder to shoulder. When educators believe that they are stronger together than they are apart, ideas seem to flow like water from a fire hose. An openness to seeking new ways to promote college readiness must be prevalent in order to experience consistent gains. Make this attitude a priority as you begin to implement your plan for promoting college readiness.

From an early age, I noticed that my parents' attitude set the tone for the choices that I would make as a youngster. When they were positive, I felt happy. When they were stressed, I felt worried. When they believed in me, I believed in me. Parent and child, teacher and student, the same holds true. All of our endeavors to transform our schools begin and end with the tone that is set by the staff. This chapter was strategically placed in this book before the chapters about students and parents because your calling as a teacher is greater than that of any other stakeholder. Your actions will be scrutinized by observant children and, more importantly, modeled by them. When a student's behavior mirrors that of a positive adult, nothing is more rewarding. No Excuses begins with the staff, but when done right it continues with students and parents.

CHAPTER EIGHT

THEORY TO PRACTICE

ITEMS FOR ARTICULATION

❏ A reason offers objective information for why a problem exists, but an excuse is made when defeat is accepted and hope is lost. What are the most common reasons for the challenges that occur for the students on your campus? What are the most popular excuses made by staff members in regard to these same students?

ITEMS FOR ACTION

❏ On a small piece of paper, during a staff meeting, have each staff member write down an excuse that they have been guilty of making. After doing so, have every member stand up, state the excuse, wad up the paper, and then throw it into a nearby trash can. As a staff, discuss the strategies that will ensure that reasons do not turn into excuses.

KEY CONCEPTS

ჸ

"The greatest danger for most of us is not that our aim is too high and we miss it, but that it is too low and we reach it."

— Michelangelo

1 Students need to be taught the difference between a job and a career.

2 The development of individual goals for every student guarantees differentiated instruction.

3 We are not in the business of discipline; we are in the business of teaching behavior.

4 The creation of a family-like atmosphere on campus is often a catalyst for teaching appropriate behavior, especially to students living in poverty.

HIGH EXPECTATIONS FOR EVERY STUDENT

From the time that I was eight years old, my Saturday mornings always began the same way. I would hear my father's footsteps enter my bedroom followed by the words "Wake up, it's time to go to work." My brother Dan and I knew that procrastination would lead to phase two of the wake-up process, when my dad would place his boot on the base of our bed and give it a solid shake that invoked a fatherly earthquake of sorts. With sleep in our eyes, we would put on our work clothes and rush downstairs for a quick breakfast before heading out to support the family business. Summer mornings were no different. When most of our friends were watching cartoons or playing outside, my brother and I were working with our father, Steve.

The family business, which was to service and install

submersible pumps for the water wells throughout our backcountry area, began as a risky endeavor on the part of my parents, who invested what little they had in the business. Because there was no money to pay a helper for my father, I guess you could say that my brother, who was ten, and I acted like two halves that made for a whole. The work each day was simple mentally, but exhausting physically. Our job was to take hundreds of feet of steel pipe out of the ground in order to replace or fix the pump at the bottom of the well. Every 21 feet, we took heavy wrenches and used them to unscrew each link of pipe. When we were done taking out all of the pipe, we replaced the pump and put it right back in. By the end of the day, our bodies were covered with dirt, rust, and grease. Our bones were achy and hands were sore from "swinging wrenches," as we called it.

As tedious as our work was, what was more repetitious during our days with my father were his teachings. Not a day went by where my dad didn't try to convince us that it was better to work with our brains than our bodies, and the only way that we could achieve that kind of work was with a college education. In order to drive the point home, my dad would often have my brother and me extend a ten-pound wrench from one arm as we held a feather-like pencil from the other. The arm with the pipe wrench would begin to shake after about 15 seconds as the weight challenged the muscles in my tiny wrist. The other arm held the pencil steadily and effortlessly. My dad's lesson: "You can graduate from high school and work with your body, or graduate from college and work with your brain." His lesson was not lost on either of us.

My father's teachings spotlighted the difference between having a job and having a career. His responsibility to us was to teach us a trade to fall back on, and also to teach us exactly what awaited us should we choose to take over the family business. Any romance that my dad had in having a "father and sons" operation was always trumped by his desire for us to have more opportunities in life than he did. He knew that a college education was a ticket into a game that he was only able to watch from the sidelines. My dad has always been a hero to me. Not just because he worked so incredibly hard to support our family, but more so because he acted selflessly in his pursuit to change a cycle of under-education that was prevalent in our previous generations.

The lessons taught to NEU students across the country from their teachers are similar to the lessons that I learned from my parents at an early age. No lesson is greater than our focus on the definitions that spotlight the difference between a job and a career. Students learn that a job is something that a person must do to earn money in order to pay for the basic needs of their families. A career, however, allows a person to be paid for doing what they, ideally, love to do. Jobs are short-lived, but careers more often than not bring with them a longevity of experiences that are personally as well as financially gratifying.

Students who live in poverty rarely get to experience the types of routines and schedules at home that model what it takes to create a career mindset. Many times, routine and structure in their daily lives occurs only within the six to eight hours they attend school each day. While many might find this fact frustrating, NEU educators see it as a gift. It's amazing how much can be accomplished within a six-hour day when caring educators assemble around a consistent message. Students who attend No Excuses Universities get a healthy dose of structure as every adult on campus consistently and reliably shares the same message. One teacher to another, one year to the next, the daily life of an NEU student is designed in such a way that he or she feels important as an individual, but also responsible for the overall success of a school community of their peers. We call that community *"the family."*

One of the first things that students learn is that they are not alone in their successes, nor their challenges. The unique value found in each student is always encouraged and built upon, as represented by the creation of individual student goals for all, but never at the cost of sacrificing the success of the family. NEU students learn that for every decision they make, both negative and positive, the effects will be felt by dozens of others as well. Because of this, students are always reminded that they are a part of a team that is bigger than themselves. As a reminder, the saying *"Don't embarrass the family. Make the family proud"* is one that is often heard on many NEU campuses. Students who come from families with similar mindsets understand all too well the importance behind these words, and those who do not are sure to learn them over the course of their tenure as NEU students. I have found that no matter the background of children or young adults, they tend to embrace this family spirit. For some, it is because they thrive on being respectful and successful ambassadors for the school. For others, it is because they feel cared for even in the midst of being disciplined on occasion. And for others, quite simply, the school is the only family that they have. Just like families, the best schools display a certain level of love, discipline, challenge, celebration, loyalty, and support. All act as a strong foundation for the work that we do to engage students in the No Excuses University experience.

BEYOND RULES

Every school in America has some form of a code of conduct that they give to students. Most contain a series of rules that let students know the expectations that adults have of them when it comes to walking in line, being respectful to adults, and exhibiting appropriate behavior to one another by keeping their hands and feet to themselves. Don't get me wrong; the fact that these rules are standard does not bother me in the least. In fact, I wholeheartedly agree and have enforced these very rules as a principal. What does rub me the wrong way, when it comes to generic student rule books, is the limitations found in many of them. Many read the same way they did when I was a kid. Some are so old that they are better displayed on stone tablets than they are on student tri-folds. They often maintain a limited focus on communicating the rules for behavior, completely bypassing the opportunities found in teaching about the habits of mind that are academic in nature. Today, our profession has access to more information than ever about student behavior, what grabs their attention, and how to communicate our expectations in a way that motivates them, yet we lean on reactive rules instead of proactive procedures. Aren't we better than this? Don't you think that our students deserve better at this point?

When the No Excuses University endeavor began, we decided that the expectations for student behavior had to be taught in harmony with our school's one goal to create academic proficiency for all. This shift in thinking made us understand that the work of student behavior was about so much more than "rules." Instead, our expectations of students were really more about a contract with them than anything else. And since a contract speaks to the need for two parties to participate, we as NEU schools promote the idea of a meaningful partnership between students and staff.

Before people sign a contract, they are informed about the expectations required of them to fulfill their obligations. Most of us have been involved in many of these situations, either as new employees signing a district contract or as new homeowners agreeing to pay back a loan. No job has ever been given to us, nor money granted on our behalf, without our signatures. Furthermore, we would never allow anyone to sign us to a contract without careful consideration on our parts. But that, unfortunately, is exactly the process that many schools use when developing a code of conduct for students.

In most cases, a *beginning-of-the-year packet* is sent out to parents containing a form about the rules that require a student's and parent's signature. These forms are returned to the school and placed in the student records file never to be seen again, unless the student misbehaves. At which point we place the form in front of the student and parent and for all intents and purposes say, "We told you so." Sure, we do a great job conveying our own liabilities with the use of forms like these, but really we do nothing to create meaningful understanding in the minds of students about the academic and behavioral expectations that we have of them. NEU schools do things differently.

During the first week of school, every grade level is asked to attend an assembly that addresses the expectations of an NEU student. We discuss the role that character plays in our school, the importance of "making the family proud," and the need for every student to live by the *code of conduct* found in the NEU handbooks given to each student. (See Appendix B.) After the assembly, teachers return to class and discuss all components of the student handbook. From learning about the consequences that may come as a result of poor character, to understanding our academic habits of mind, to charting progress in a variety of assessments, this handbook acts as a guide for a student's college readiness journey. After students have been thoroughly informed about the handbook, they are asked to sign our NEU Three-Way Pledge. (See Appendix B.)

This process of developing a foundational understanding in the area of expectations is certainly more involved than some might like. However, we find that the amount of time that has been invested proactively teaching students at the beginning of the year saves us tenfold in reactive measures that need to be taken by the end of the year.

Student Goals

The term "differentiated instruction" may be the most overused cliché in the business. When asked how a teacher supports the individual needs of each student, the response is almost always that they "differentiate instruction." For many, this may be true, but for far more it is not. It has nothing to do with teachers not knowing how to differentiate or even being lazy. It is incredibly hard to differentiate instruction for every student in a class. The more our pedagogy evolves, the more we understand just how important it is to capitalize on the strengths and attack the weaknesses of every student. In a classroom of 20 or 30 students, the chances that all children are performing at the same level with the same strengths are nearly impossible. Because of this, No Excuses Universities create individual goals for every student in the school.

What began as an idea to help support the most at-risk students in our school quickly became a comprehensive effort to promote academic growth for all. The teachers at Los Peñasquitos Elementary led an effort that became one of, if not the most, substantial reason for our school's success. Teachers decided that as part of a school-wide assessment commitment, we would use formative assessments to hone in on the individual needs of students. No longer would we discuss a student's weakness in the subject of "math;" rather, we talked about their lack of growth in the area of problem solving. Instead of saying that students were "below grade level" in reading, we sought to find better strategies to bring them up to par in the area of literal comprehension. The fine-tuning of our efforts to spotlight the subcategories within the curriculum made all the difference in the world.

As part of an assessment commitment endorsed by the entire staff, students create individual goals with their teachers at least three times a year. These goals are data specific and representative of a partnership between the student and the teacher. No longer do teachers call students to the back of the room to participate in an assessment that the kids know nothing about. The student goal process requires that teachers share the details about the assessment, how it is scored, and why it important in the creation of an individual goal. Through this process, students begin to learn about the importance of assessment and how to analyze the data.

After quality assessments have been given, the teacher

works to spotlight the greatest learning need that exists for each student. Teachers then hold conferences with the students to create goals. Each conference may look a little different depending on the grade or the teacher, but every goal should include the following components:

1. *Students should only create one goal at a time.* We have found that more than one goal gets forgotten by students and teachers. Teachers are often tempted to create goals for students in each subject area; however, we must remember that the student goal process is about quality, not quantity.

2. *Each goal must contain tangible steps that help students improve in their goal area.* Steps such as "try harder" or "read more" do nothing to support kids. Teachers are encouraged to collaboratively generate ideas as a team in an effort to accumulate an abundance of strategies to pass on to students. Quality goals offer three to four different strategies or ideas that students can use to improve, but no more.

3. *Students should be given visible access to their goals on a daily basis.* Some classrooms post goals on the wall, while others have designated goals folders. Many primary-aged students have their goals taped to the top of their desks. However you decide to display your goals, remember that students will care about them only as much as you do. Teachers who rarely reference goals tend to have students who forget them.

4. *Goals must be academic in nature.* There may be a need for some students to have behavior goals, but this should be in addition to a well-thought-out academic goal.

As a principal, one of my most common conversations with students revolved around goals. During these conversations, I would ask the students three very important questions:

"What is your goal?" Students' answers to these questions showed their investment and commitment in the process.

"What are you doing to help achieve your goal?" These answers expressed their plans for reaching their goals.

"How will you know when you have met your goal?" These answers demonstrated that their goals were data-specific.

Of the numerous conversations that I had with students, I was always amazed at the ability of a six-, seven-, or eight-year-old to understand the concept of goal-setting. In addition, I was regularly astonished at how goals helped to improve the individual and school-wide achievement of our students.

Many educators wonder how to get students invested in the learning process. The answer is crystal clear: Create individual goals with them. When you do, you do away with the cliché of differentiation and guarantee that every student in your school is being taught at his or her level. One of the greatest misperceptions about Los Peñasquitos Elementary's success is that the staff focused all of their efforts on "teaching to the test." The fact is that our teachers, and the teachers at successful No Excuses Universities, focus on individual growth for all. When you maintain such a focus, test scores tend to take care of themselves.

The dreams that NEU staff members hold for our students are often bigger than the students themselves can comprehend. I, like many of you, am living proof of the importance of having others help stimulate those dreams throughout a lifetime. For me, it was my parents. The conversations that took place in my childhood about college eventually led to a very real *rite of passage* when I was 18. I will never forget the first day that my parents moved me into my dorm room. A young small-town boy with the propensity for being homesick, I stood in a 10x10 room and asked myself, "Will I even make it past the first semester?"

As I said goodbye to my parents and my younger sister Aubrey, the answer to that question could not have been clearer. While other students were handed keys to brand-new cars as a gift for their hard work in being accepted to college, my father pulled from his pocket an equally special offering to me. It was a small, and very rusty, version of the same pipe wrench that my brother and I used to "swing" growing up. It moved me, not because of its tangible nature, but because of my father's words accompanying the tool. He looked me in the eyes and said, "If you ever decide that college isn't for you, I will support you 100%. But be sure to let this wrench act as a reminder of what waits for you when you come home." He hugged me and waved good-bye. That was all he needed to say. To this day, the wrench hangs proudly in my office.

CHAPTER NINE
THEORY TO PRACTICE

ITEMS FOR ARTICULATION

❏ The key to getting students invested in the assessment process is to work closely with them. As a team, discuss specific examples of how you have made students your partners in the area of assessment. Ask yourself: "Do my students understand the nature of each assessment, why we give them assessments, and what each score means to them?"

ITEMS FOR ACTION

Creating individual goals is vital to our commitment to differentiate instruction for each student. Schools should experiment in this process through the following steps.

❏ *Step One:* Have each teacher select three at-risk students and create one student goal with each.

❏ *Step Two:* Take the time over the course of six to eight weeks to discuss the progress of your students with your team.

❏ *Step Three:* As a team and a school, decide upon a timeline for rolling out the goals process so that it affects every student on campus.

Note: Most schools take between six months and a year to experiment and learn about the goals process before they implement it school-wide. This is not to say that it can't be done in less time; it is simply to advise schools to take time to implement the process in a quality manner from the start.

KEY CONCEPTS

"*If kids come to us [educators/teachers] from strong, healthy functioning families, it makes our job easier. If they do not come to us from strong, healthy, functioning families, it makes our job more important.*"

— Barbara Colorose

1 Demanding responsible parenting from those who were never taught such skills is futile.

2 Schools need to focus on the individual needs of families through differentiated parenting support.

3 The more secure parents are in the relationships they have with teachers, the more likely they are to take advice from the school.

PARTNERING WITH PARENTS

I have learned over time that no matter how convincing I think I may be when offering professional development to educators, there's always at least one person who finds a flaw in the message. While working with an elementary school staff in California, I saw this firsthand. As I presented information about the beliefs associated with creating a culture of universal achievement, a young teacher raised her hand and shared her frustration: "I would have 100% proficiency in my class if it weren't for just one of my kids!"

I asked her why this one student was not at grade-level standards. She simply said, "Because of the parents."

The voices in the room cried out with approval as heads nodded up and down to share their agreement with the teacher. I went on to inquire, "What is it about these parents that cause this particular student to fail?"

Among her litany of reasons were "they never help him on homework, they never read with him at home, they never volunteer in the classroom, they never drive on field trips...."

I stopped her and asked, "Why don't they do any of those things?"

She replied, "Because they are both addicted to drugs; they're methamphetamine addicts."

There was silence in the room before I finally said, "Let me ask you something. Why do you want two meth addicts driving on a field trip?"

She had nothing more to say. My candor forced her to look inwardly for the lack of results that she was getting from this one young boy. She had rationalized his lack of success based on a number of excuses with a victim mentality that, in the end, did nothing to improve the academic status of her student. In doing so, she pointed her finger squarely at the parents, an act that is easily done by many educators experiencing frustration.

As a former teacher, I remember the challenges that went along with teaching students who came from home environments that were less than ideal. As a principal, I have worked with dozens of abused children who live challenging existences that most of us will never truly understand. In both roles I have found that blaming parents for lackluster performance, both academically and behaviorally, is one of the easiest things in the world to do. I have experienced times when these excuses made educators feel better about their own limitations for garnering results, but didn't do a damn thing to change the reality of the current situation for the student. Is it true that poor parenting makes our job harder? Of course it is, but dwelling on this fact without seeking timely solutions is a luxury that we simply do not have in public education. You and I could name a child who went from one grade to the next where teachers used the same excuse for why he or she was failing. Before we know it, six, seven, eight years pass by in this student's career with the same excuses ... and the same results. How do we move beyond our frustrations and into proactive solutions regarding parenting support? We make them partners in our college readiness endeavor.

The term "parents as partners" has become an overused pledge in our profession. Such a term is now expected to be part of district mission statements and school improvement plans. I question whether or not those who write such statements truly seek to implement the goals associated with them. I have visited many schools that had value statements regarding parents as partners that were upbeat and supportive, but attitudes about parents that were negative and critical. I have no doubt that these schools would like nothing more than to have their deeds match their words. They just don't know how to connect with them in a way that unifies their support with the purpose of the school.

The No Excuses University endeavor makes it easy for parents to understand, support, and participate in the goals of a school. This is done in two very important ways. First, we publicize our expectations to parents in a way that is respectful, timely, and clear. Second, rather than demand participation from parents, we seek to get them more involved in the workings of the school by reaching out to their basic needs. Both steps have helped us to create a more positive climate for students, parents, and staff members.

PUBLICIZING TO PARENTS

When I became the principal of Los Peñasquitos Elementary School, there were two looming concerns involving the parents within our community. The first had to do with attendance. Not unlike other schools, the numbers showed that our attendance on Mondays and Fridays was significantly lower than that during the rest of the week. While the majority of our parents did an outstanding job of getting their children to school on time, others did not view their son's or daughter's education as a priority and it showed in the extended weekend plans that were made with little to no regard for what the students were missing at school. Because the school is close to the Mexican border and had a large Hispanic population at the time, many of our parents were going home to visit families and returning at their own pace. While we could not judge the rationale for or the necessity of taking these trips outside of the country, we as a school determined that it was harming the success of our students.

The second concern in regard to parent involvement had to do with the safety of our campus. Like many campuses, ours was an open campus that allowed anyone unfettered access to our school grounds. Sure, there were signs informing all visitors to check in through the office, but more times than not, people ignored them. It was the culture of the school to allow our parents to roam freely. But the tragic events of September 11, 2001 changed everything and modifications were not only necessary; they were required. Immediately, we began locking the gates to our school, allowing only one entrance to our campus, which went through the school office. In addition, all visitors were required to show ID to the school secretary. To my surprise, this measure infuriated some parents who had left their identification in the car. They felt inconvenienced by the fact that they were asked to return to the parking lot to retrieve their drivers' licenses.

Both attendance and school safety concerns became the only two non-negotiable items that I had with parents. I went out of my way to publicize this fact to each parent in writing, phone calls, and face-to-face conversations. When a parent began to show frustration to my office staff members, I stepped in and candidly explained our check-in procedure without apology. When students consistently missed school due to reasons other than illness, I did everything in my power to let the parents know that this was unacceptable. From walking to apartments and homes in order to speak with parents directly, to involving our district truant officer, I would stop at nothing to create a cultural shift in the eyes of our community. After about a year, I realized that my efforts were paying off. Attendance numbers began to improve, but more importantly, the attitudes of parents began to change. While walking across the street in one of our apartment complexes, I overhead a parent say to another, "Whatever you do, don't mess with Lopez when it comes to getting your kid to school. It's not worth it." The parent went on to share about how I filled up her voicemail box with messages and finally called her at work to talk about her son's attendance.

These examples represent mountains that are worthy of climbing. Unfortunately, some schools pick far too many issues to focus on with parents. Some demand that homework is completed appropriately, placing the burden on both the student and the parent. Others decide that classroom participation or financial support must take place in order to fund school projects or even parties. These demands come with great opposition from parents who are simply trying to make it through the day. After hearing numerous complaints from the school over a variety of items, our words become little more than background noise to parents, who inevitably throw up their hands and say, "Forget it!" I've learned along the way, sometimes the hard way, that picking your battles is a virtue that proves to be invaluable as a principal.

Just as important as picking your battles is knowing when to make your stand. From the beginning of our No Excuses University endeavor, we have made it a point to have every parent attend an NEU Parent Forum. These forums present the work that we are doing around college readiness, how parents can participate if they wish, and what is expected of each of them when it comes to our two non-negotiables. In our first year conducting these forums, parents were given five different opportunities to attend. The meetings took place on campus and typically lasted 45 minutes or less. After about 80% of our parents showed up, we scheduled two more forums in an effort to ensure that every student would have a parent attend. After this, we were left with a handful of parents who had yet to attend this mandated meeting. In a last-ditch effort to get parents involved, I sent out a letter along with voicemail messages that said:

Dear Parents,

As you may recall, we sent out a letter inviting you to attend one of the seven NEU Parent Forum meetings held over the course of the last several weeks. Because it is a requirement to attend, we wanted to schedule these meetings during a variety of days and times so that you might be able to join us. Unfortunately, your child has yet to be represented by a parent at one of these meetings. In an effort to go the extra mile, we have scheduled one more meeting for you to attend on September 23rd at 6 pm. If you cannot attend, please know that we will be scheduling a home visit with you in an effort to present this important information to you face to face. The No Excuses University endeavor is one that is exciting for all involved. We know that greater success will be realized if all

students, parents, and staff have a true understanding about
this work. I look forward to seeing you at our next meeting!

> *Sincerely,*
> *Damen Lopez*
> *Principal*

To no one's surprise, the vast majority of parents showed up to that final meeting. However, I do recall making several visits alongside our school counselor, Fran Hjalmarson, to apartments and houses with my laptop in hand. This took a lot of time, but it was well worth it as we laid the groundwork for publicizing our college readiness initiative. As part of our NEU Parent Forum, we focused our message on ways that parents could be encouraged to support their children and the school. In turn, we also shared ways that the schools would support parents.

Just as every teacher created an individual goal unique to each student, we encouraged parents to create unique parenting goals for themselves. These goals would speak directly to the ways that parents would help support their child's academic progress. In addition, every goal would note ways in which moms and dads could continue to grow as parents. When parents create goals for themselves, they assume a level of accountability in a manner that mirrors that of their own child. And because they are seeking ways to improve as parents, they model supportive behavior that connects directly with our college readiness initiative. (See Appendix B.)

In addition to parenting goals, we encourage all parents to take part in a daily conversation with their children referred to as "Take Five." This conversation, focusing on five questions, is designed to be simple and last no more than five minutes. Some parents begin their Take Five conversation while walking home from school, while others engage in dialogue on their ride home in the car. Still others use the Take Five template to guide their talk at home. After attending the NEU Parent Forum, each family is given a magnet with our five key questions on it to put on their refrigerators. This small gift both encourages parents to have daily conversations with their students and also reinforces a similar culture at home that we try hard to instill at school.

TAKE FIVE

1. What is your student goal?

2. What did you do today to help achieve your student goal?

3. How did you make character count today?

4. What can you do tomorrow to conduct yourself as a No Excuses University Student?

5. Encourage your child in a very specific and genuine way.

Finally, when it comes to publicizing our college readiness focus to parents, each grade level creates Parent Assessment Guides that offer detailed information about the types of tests that students will be taking. In addition, they provide the contact information of every teacher should a parent wish to seek further information regarding assessment. For years, we hesitated sharing such information, not because we wanted to hide it, but more so because we assumed that our large second-language parent population would not understand. This assumption may have been correct in many cases, but it was no excuse for not doing our best to communicate the value that we placed on using data-driven assessments to target the individual needs of students. These guides were simple to create and easy to distribute. Some parents read them, others did not, but most of them appreciated our attempt to go the extra mile in an effort to provide better communication.

DIFFERENTIATED PARENTING SUPPORT

The second major way that we make parents our partners in the NEU endeavor is through what we call "Differentiated Parenting Support." This style of support acts as a form of outreach to our parents, who bring with them a plethora of needs based on their individual circumstances. The brainchild of Fran Hjalmarson, an author and our school counselor, this method of supporting parents is actually an exceptional system of sorts that has impacted the culture of our school in significant ways.

The idea of Differentiated Parenting Support came as a result of 25 years of unproductive efforts to engage our parent community in the goals of our school. For years, we demanded that parents participate in homework, volunteer on site, and exemplify the definition of "parent." The problem was that many of our parents were either so incredibly busy keeping their heads above water that they couldn't do any of these things, or had come from environments where they were not taught the skills that you and I find second nature as parents. Of course they loved their kids; there was no doubt about that. But they did not grasp the obligation that a parent has as a partner with the school.

For years, I, along with several other staff members and fellow parents, pondered why this was the case. It wasn't until Fran joined our team in 2003 that we finally understood the answer. We had been trying to treat every parent the same way, when all along we should have been treating them as individuals. I remember one day in my office Fran saying, "We differentiate our support for students; why aren't we doing the same for our parents?"

It was an "aha" moment for all of us. Immediately, Fran began working with a small team of staff members, seeking to systematically support parents in a whole new way. Instead of waiting for parents to come to the school in search of support, we began to go directly to them. When we found out that a family was struggling financially, we would partner with faith-based organizations in order to provide essential items like food or clothing. When we learned that dozens of families could not afford a Thanksgiving meal, we worked with a sister school to provide a feast with all the trimmings. When Christmas came and there was little chance of some of our students having presents under the tree, we leaned on our local police unit to put together a party for our most needy children. No matter the need or the reason, Fran and the staff found a way to reach out to our parents. Through it all, we never got caught up in the frustration of the circumstances that came as a result of the poor decisions that some of our parents made in their lives. We focused on the fact that these parents needed a friend in the school. The volunteers and staff members who did not offer their support for the sake of the parents were compelled to do so instead out of their love for the kids.

As extraordinary as this shift in thinking was, what was more exciting was the outcome of our work. Parents who never used to show their faces on campus came often to seek support for various reasons. And because they were on campus more, they were more in touch with the academic and behavior status of their children. If their children were having difficulties, these parents were far more eager to be supportive. Many times however, because of our outreach, parents found out about positive results that were taking place with their kids and about the amount of care that the school had for the individual wellbeing of their children. This made them swell with pride and encouraged them to be more invested in the partnership that we were trying to promote.

The more parents became comfortable with the school, the more likely they were to learn and take advice from staff members. Fran and her team took advantage of this newfound interest within our parent community and created the No Excuses Parent University. This collection of courses was a form of professional development for parents. As we used to say, "Come and get your master's in parenting." The Parent University offered free sessions to adults, and sometimes their children, that took place on campus in the evening. Several staff members taught courses such as Family Math Night, where parents learned ways to enhance and support math skills with their children at home. Other sessions, like Developing Capable Young People (based on the work of H. Stephen Glenn), were taught by trained individuals like Fran who dug deep into meaningful strategies that parents could use to promote lifelong success skills for their kids. From police officers who taught safety courses, to specialists who supported literacy development, the courses that made up the Parent University program were well received. But it wasn't just the variety of options that we offered to parents that made it successful; it was the way in which we reached out to parents to encourage them to participate.

I've met some educators who believe that parents lacking basic parenting skills should be required to go to classes like the ones we offered through the Parent University. Those who force this requirement on parents are likely to get a negative and defensive response. And who would blame parents? No adult wants to be told that he or she needs to improve in the area of parenting. It's humiliating. We understood this at Los Pen and took a different approach to filling the seats of our classes. Instead of telling parents that they needed to participate, we publicized our events by asking parents to attend alongside staff members. In one instance, I attended a Developing Capable Young People (DCYP) workshop. I went around beforehand sharing my plan to attend with other parents whom I felt could benefit as well. I would walk up to one of the parents and say something like, "Because I have kids of my own, I'm going to attend DCYP classes. You should join me and we can learn together." On other occasions, I might encourage parents to attend by sharing how their parenting experiences could add a lot to the conversation. We found that any anxieties or defensiveness that parents might feel in attending classes like these were neutralized when staff members were inviting and made the choice to associate with parents not as teachers, but as fellow parents.

The work of the Parent University at Los Pen can be found in similar forms throughout the NEU Network of Schools. Educators within our network understand the need to reach out to our parents in unique and different ways. Schools like the No Excuses University at Vermont Elementary School in San Bernardino, California have made amazing steps forward to shift their school culture. An exemplary model that supports parents, Vermont Parent University (VPU) has an abundance of learning opportunities featured in a yearly course catalog. (See Appendix B). This catalog offers engaging classes that are free to every school parent. The effects of this program were felt immediately. Liz Atkinson, principal of NEU at Vermont, offered her thoughts about VPU: "I have noticed several significant changes to the culture of Vermont School since the creation and implementation of Vermont Parent University. First, parents have built a stronger rapport with our teachers through a common understanding of what is expected in our classrooms. They aren't afraid to ask questions or admit that they need help in a particular area. Second, parents feel much more confident in their abilities to help their children with their homework. Finally, our students show pride in their parents' interest in life-long learning. Our parents wear VPU shirts on the VPU class days to emulate their desire to be better-educated adults. In our inaugural year, we graduated 120 parents from Vermont Parent University who are now equipped to facilitate learning for their children at home."

Schools that wish to embrace parents as partners must first choose to shift their own thinking. The Vermont Parent University is a perfect example of productive change as a result of such a shift. There are always times for us as educators to be firm in our expectations of parents, but we must choose our stances wisely and do so with respect. Our understandings about the circumstances that many parents deal with on a daily basis should always be taken into account when sharing expectations with our parent community. We have found that there is a middle ground between enabling and commanding our parents. That middle ground is found in the way that we reach out to support the needs of our families.

In my career thus far, I have had the privilege to hear many very kind words from educators who have attended my conferences or visited schools in the network. Even so, the nicest thing that was ever said to me came from a complete stranger in one of the most unexpected of places. One day while sitting on the beach with my wife and kids, a stranger noticed the collective work that we were engaged in as we were playing on the shore. My girls were multi-tasking, both building a sand castle and dumping the leftover sand on my wife's legs and in my hair. As this stranger came upon us, she stopped briefly, looked me in the eyes and said, "You have a really nice family."

I thanked her and she continued her walk down the beach. After she left, my heart was filled with gratitude for her words and pride in my family. I did not know this woman, but the words that she used to compliment my kids were enough to make me feel honored. Those of you who are parents know that when someone says kind things about your kids, in many respects, they're saying kind things about you. In fact, if given the choice, most parents would rather hear compliments about their children than receive accolades about themselves. As we work to strengthen our partnership with parents, we must never forget that no matter how unqualified we perceive parents to be, in their heart of hearts they love their kids far more than any of us ever could. We must never, ever assume that we know better or care more for children then their own parents do. The best defense against such an attitude is to show a level of caring towards parents that is akin to the commitment we show to students in the classroom. When we do this, parents will not only learn the values that we promote through our No Excuses University endeavor; they will embrace them as well.

CHAPTER TEN

THEORY TO PRACTICE

ITEMS FOR ARTICULATION

❏ Think about your families living in poverty. When was the last time your teammates or you visited the homes or apartments of these families? Why might this be important?

ITEMS FOR ACTION

❏ As a school, choose a day to visit the homes or apartments of some of your neediest families. During your brief visits, say a kind word to the parents about their children, drop off a small treat as part of a holiday, or deliver information about an upcoming event. No matter how you choose to reach out to parents, make this a time that your staff displays a unified spirit of caring and stewardship.

KEY CONCEPTS

⚷

"Coming together is a beginning. Keeping together is progress. Working together is success."

— Henry Ford

1 No Excuses University schools partner with universities throughout the world in an effort to bring the reality of college to life for students.

2 Partnerships are created over time between the classroom teacher and various university representatives.

3 Elementary schools should focus on four-year universities.

4 Students should learn more about community college options in middle school and trade school options in high school.

UNIVERSITY PARTNERSHIPS

The creation of the No Excuses University endeavor prompted immediate interest from educators throughout the country. Phone calls and emails from those in search of information became a daily occurrence for us. Principals contacted me seeking strategies to help them begin the process at their schools. Teachers asked how they too could create meaningful partnerships with universities. On many occasions, it was the universities themselves who called to offer support. The response was overwhelmingly positive, which is why I was so stunned one day when I received an odd request from a gentleman named Craig.

It didn't take me long to sense his frustration. Immediately after I introduced myself on the phone, Craig voiced his distaste for what he was viewing on the Los Pen website. He

159

said, "I went online today and looked at your website. After about five seconds, I was disgusted with what I saw on the home page."

Worried that I had somehow overlooked a glaring mistake and expecting the worst, I said, "Please, tell me what's wrong and I'd be happy to fix it."

"On your website is a picture of three really cute kids. Unfortunately, they're wearing the most offensive t-shirts I have ever seen in my life."

"Really?" I asked.

"Yes. Those kids are wearing shirts from the University of Michigan. I'm from Michigan State. How do I get that blue and gold off your site and Michigan State green on instead?"

After a huge sigh of relief, I laughed and said, "Hey man, if you want Michigan State represented, you need to come and adopt one of our classrooms."

Sure enough, Craig showed up a couple of weeks later with brand new t-shirts for Mrs. Gentry's third-grade class. He spoke to the students about his experiences, taught them the Michigan State fight song, and encouraged them to keep working hard. It was clear that his visit not only inspired the students, but excited him as well.

Before departing, Craig dropped by my office, placed his hand on my shoulder, and said, "OK, Mr. Lopez. What do I need to do to get you to stack the Michigan State class with the smartest kids in the school next year?"

I asked, "Why would I want to do that, Craig?"

"Because I want Michigan State to beat Michigan in everything they do."

I jokingly made an appeal for his understanding. "Michigan State is third grade; Michigan is second grade. I love your competitive spirit, but I think you need to relax a bit."

The partnerships that No Excuses University classrooms have built with hundreds of college representatives are as exciting as the one that Craig has forged with Mrs. Gentry's third-grade class. From Boise State football players dropping off a sample of their bright blue "Smurf Turf" at a school in Los Angeles, to the Illinois State University mascot "Reggie the Redbird" visiting a NEU campus in Chicago, the stories of successful partnerships are plenty. Such exposure to tangible models of college makes the concept very real to students and provides a source of encouragement for kids, allowing them to set their sights high on the goal of earning a university degree. "The kids feel like they are part of something," said third-grade NEU teacher Debra Baadilla in a recent Press-Enterprise article. "They all know when they are going to college and what year they're going to graduate."

With dozens of No Excuses Universities participating as part of our official network of schools, we have been able to learn a lot about how to create beneficial partnerships between colleges and classrooms. As you seek to open the doors to collaboration with colleges and universities, take a look at the answers to some of the most commonly asked questions regarding university partnerships.

What makes a good partnership?

A quality partnership with a college or university is one that is beneficial to both parties. Universities love partnerships because of the publicity and the ability to spread the word about the benefits of their campuses to future students. Teachers and students love the partnership because of the free college gear and visits from alumni. I would suggest that teachers first seek to build a collaborative link between a university representative and themselves. Calling or writing with the sole purpose of getting "stuff" is likely a turn-off and defeats the purpose. The best partnerships are those that are built over time.

Kerri Kutzner, a teacher in San Diego, began the partnership between her fourth-grade class and the University of Nebraska simply by sharing what NEU was all about. She corresponded with the university and was very open-ended about the variety of ways that a partnership could help. What began as a box of pencils and information packets about the university has become something much bigger. To date, her students have received t-shirts, pennants, inspirational letters from staff members, signed books by famous alumni, and surprise visits from football players. While this was never the end goal, Kerri's continuous partnership with the university has grown in such a way that the employees of the university are as excited as the kids are about the process. Partnerships are made over the course of several months, not several weeks. Be patient as you go forward. In the event that you are unable to grasp the interest of a particular university, select a different one. With more than 4,000 colleges and universities across the country, there's more than enough to choose from.

How can we encourage universities to become partners?

The first step in creating a partnership is to inform universities about the work that you are doing. We chose to send letters to alumni presidents who lived in our area. Creating a partnership with alumni organizations is key; they are the most capable of supporting your needs. Some schools and classrooms have successfully partnered directly with a university, but those partnerships tend to be ones that involved local universities and colleges. While I would never discourage people from trying to find representatives at all levels, I would suggest you save direct university contacts as your last resort. My hope is that the NEU model will gain influence in the future and in turn garner more direct support from universities. Until then, it is best to disperse our requests in a variety of ways so as to not overwhelm any one sector of the university system.

Once you have selected your contact, a simple letter or email is always the best avenue to introduce your interest in a partnership. (A sample can be found in Appendix B.) Remember, as described in chapter 13, only schools that have officially joined the NEU Network of Schools can use the trademarked name and logo.

Which universities are the best to choose?

I couldn't be happier with the feedback that I have received from universities that are partnering with our NEU endeavor. Their generosity is beyond any initial hopes that I had when this work began. A shining example of that support can be found in the generous involvement of the Wake Forest Alumni Association. After experiencing a terrific partnership with one of our NEU classes in Hemet, California, a representative contacted me directly asking how the university could expand its support. Because of this, numerous classrooms are now experiencing the joy of learning about this terrific university and the options that are available to students who attend. Partnerships like these are not unique. Rather than suggest which specific universities a teacher should pursue, I would much rather describe the types of universities classes should seek to create partnerships with.

The work of exposing students to colleges and universities is one of the most enjoyable features of the NEU model. However, you should always be aware of the end message that you wish to send to students. No Excuses Universities have a plan to expose students to the right opportunities at the appropriate times. For elementary schools, we focus on promoting four-year colleges and universities. These universities are typically selected because of easy access to college flags, banners, and apparel, or due to a personal connection that educators have as alumni. The selection of four-year universities at the elementary level is purposeful. It is too early for us to suggest that students have any limitations on their potential to earn bachelor's, master's, or even doctoral degrees when they grow up. Might some of them take the community college track? Of course, and of course there is nothing wrong with them doing so. But when it comes to setting early expectations for students, you always want to place the bar as high as possible. The statistics, as you will see, show a much higher completion rate when students strive for a four-year degree.

When it comes to middle school or junior high, we encourage schools to begin featuring several community colleges throughout their campus. Why wait until middle school? Because the data supports such a decision. In 2007, *USA Today* reported that only 51% of all students who enrolled in a community college for the first year returned for a second year. This is far less than the 69% of four-year university freshmen who returned for their sophomore year. In addition, among the community college students who did return, only 36% received an associate's or bachelor's degree after six years of attendance. The message sent regarding community college at any level should be one that focuses on utilizing this route as a *means* to a four-year degree. Junior high and middle school is the best time to help create this message.

The issue of trade schools comes up quite often. As a son of a blue-collar worker, I am fully aware of the ability of individuals to attend trade schools and make an excellent living for themselves. These people support their families and make up a section of our population that should be respected and appreciated. In no way should we thumb our noses at trade schools. That said, the time for such discussion should not take place until students enter high school. Five-year-olds who want to enter a welding school can make that decision when they are fifteen or sixteen just as easily. Should they decide to go this route after several years of information about the greater benefits of a college education, then we can support them with the knowledge that we exposed them to every possibility. The idea of attending college is one that must be planned out for many years, while the decision to attend a trade school can be made within a much shorter time span. This method is the safest way for us to keep all doors of possibility open for students from all types of backgrounds.

What is the impact of college partnerships on parents?

If you would have asked me during the birth of NEU what my number one concern would be in promoting college readiness, I would have shared my concern for how the parents would respond. I was worried that parents without college degrees would take offense and challenge my leadership. Boy was I wrong. In the many years that I have been involved with this endeavor, I have had only two negative opinions shared with me from parents. One of those opinions came from a very wealthy parent who wasn't frustrated by the fact that we were discussing college, but instead was angry that we were allowing all of the students to participate. I guess she would rather that we only provide the opportunity to the most "gifted" kids in the school.

Loons like this parent aside, I cannot begin to count how many parents have come up to me and said, "Thank you for sharing this message with my child, one that I was not credible enough to deliver to them myself." The support has been overwhelming. The parents have just as much fun portraying the college spirit as the students do. On any given Monday or Friday, parents are just as likely to have NEU or college gear on as their children. When college football or basketball season rolls around, parents are more engaged than ever as they root for a particular university right beside their kids. This creates a unifying spirit, but more importantly brings students and parents together in ways that benefit the home environment as much as it does the school surroundings. No story exemplifies this better than one that involved a young first-grade boy and his grandmother.

The only son of Iranian immigrants, Navid was a first grader at Los Pen who actively sought to honor his parents by working hard in school. One Monday morning, I noticed Navid hopping up and down on one leg as a result of what appeared to be an injury over the weekend. After watching him struggle to make it from one end of the campus to the other, I called him to the nurse's office to find out what had happened. Navid, wearing his No Excuses University t-shirt, winced as he sat down on a chair.

"What happened?" I asked.

He said he had badly sprained his ankle while playing outside. When I asked if he had seen a doctor, he answered, "Yes. He told me that it would get better in a few days. I'm supposed to stay off of my ankle until Wednesday."

Proud of his tenacity to fight through the pain, I inquired, "If the doctor told you to stay off of your ankle, why did you come to school today?"

Immediately he exclaimed, "No Excuses, Mr. Lopez!"

As touched as I was by his loyal commitment to our motto, I explained to Navid that a doctor's recommendations trump those of a principal. I told him that I would need to call his grandmother, who took care of him during the day, and have her pick him up.

Navid's grandmother, who arrived within minutes wearing her No Excuses University t-shirt, came into the office with a concerned look on her face. Speaking only Farsi, she pointed her finger at Navid as if to scold him. After some back and forth took place within their native language, I asked, "Navid, what is your grandmother saying?"

He said, "Mr. Lopez, she wants to know if it would be OK for her to carry me around school all day so that I don't miss class."

This kind of commitment by a grandparent is the definition of the effect that No Excuses University has on the families within our network.

What do we do after we have created partnerships?

As shared in previous chapters, there is an abundance of opportunities to pursue when it comes to promoting colleges and universities. From each classroom creating a college chant, to grade levels visiting college campuses, the continued exposure to all things college is key. Many NEU schools have developed yearly college fairs that bring in local universities and guest speakers. This provides a wonderful opportunity for students to learn not only about their own adopted university, but also other universities as well. Highly collaborative classes that work together will certainly develop several ideas that take your partnerships to the next level. As you work to develop a greater understanding about college for your students, don't forget to focus also on what it takes to get there. The older students get, the more involved you should be in sharing the steps that one must take to apply, enroll, and qualify for acceptance into the university system.

Dr. David Conley's book *College Knowledge: What It Really Takes for Students to Succeed and What We Can Do to Get Them Ready,* while written with a secondary focus, is a wealth of information for parents and teachers seeking to set their students up for success. "Many students are unable to attend college not because of their grades, but instead because they have not been able to navigate through this very challenging system," Dr. Conley said in a recent interview with me. Because many young adults do not know the difference between two and four-year colleges, he said, "it is the job of the adults to make this clear."

Dr. Conley's research has created a path for many students, especially high school students, to follow. His declaration that "educators and other adults have a profound impact on the success rate of college acceptance" aligns directly with our work with the No Excuses University.

The partnerships between classrooms and universities spotlighted in this chapter provide insight into the possibilities that exist when post-secondary educators align their passions with K-12 staff members. The feedback I have received from university representatives convinces me that they are both willing and eager to lend a hand. With the successful collaborative relationships being built between NEU schools and university campuses today, I can only imagine where our movement will be several years from now.

THEORY TO PRACTICE

ITEMS FOR ARTICULATION

❏ When was the first time you visited a college campus? How did that visit influence your view of higher education?

❏ What would an ideal partnership between a university and your classroom look like? What steps might you take to create such a partnership?

ITEMS FOR ACTION

One of the best ways to bring college readiness to life through university partnerships is to create a college fair. As a school, work with university partners, parents, and community members to design a day-long college fair that exposes students to a variety of college options. Some activities to consider:

❏ Solicit guest speakers to deliver inspirational

messages to individual grade levels about their own college experiences.

❑ Have students rotate through a series of college readiness activities.

❑ Invite university representatives to set up booths that offer information about their campuses.

❑ Allow students to design and share college displays in the same manner as a science fair.

The possibilities are endless when you collaborate with passionate educators.

KEY CONCEPTS

♀

"Greatness is not a function of circumstance. Greatness, it turns out, is largely a matter of conscious choice, and discipline."

— Jim Collins

1 The NEU endorsement acts as a playbook of sorts that helps to guide a school's path.

2 Every system created by a staff is displayed in a practitioner-friendly way.

3 Schedules, strategies, and agreements within the endorsement are explicit.

4 The endorsement is revised and signed by the staff each year in an effort to meet the changing needs of students.

THE NEU ENDORSEMENT: A STAFF'S PROMISE

Like many who grow up in a small town, I found the experience to be enjoyable as a young boy, but challenging by the time I entered high school. The romance of living in an Andy Griffith-like community became tainted by the reality of the trials that I faced as a teenager. The greatest challenge of all was the fact that I attended school with very few individuals who had a like-minded perspective about the future. Normally, students who face such challenges take comfort in the support that they receive from their teachers. For me, however, that demographic happened to be the one that presented most of the challenges.

I did, like most students, have a handful of highly supportive adults in high school who genuinely cared for me

175

and actively sought out the good in me when my attitude or work habits were not all that they should have been. Among the best was my typing teacher, Mr. Wynn. His structured teaching and flexible understanding got the best out of me without breaking my spirit. As great as he was, the subject matter that he taught was not exactly what universities were looking for in future alumni from their school. Absent my ability to type 85 words a minute, I partook in a high school education that left me ill-prepared academically and under-encouraged socially. Enter Ms. Leystan.

Ms. Leystan, whose name is fictional but whose presence was all too real, left a mark on my high school career that has yet to be forgotten. Her demeaning treatment of the young adult in me created a motivation out of spite for her that in many ways helped shape me into the man I am today. Ms. Leystan and I were about as different as they come. The personal beliefs about education that she openly shared with my classmates and I were nowhere near the ones that I held as an individual. I cannot recall a time when she mentioned the word "college" and if she did, it certainly was not used as a suggested path for any of us to follow. And while I can think of a dozen reasons why Ms. Leystan represented everything that I dislike in a teacher, it was her view of education itself that makes me cringe to this day.

Ms. Leystan had a simple perspective when it came to delivering instruction. She felt that it was her job to teach, and it was my job to learn. Strategies of motivating students to learn or building on the individual strengths that they possess must have been taught in a course that she chose to sleep through in pursuit of her own college degree. When I was challenged by the content, the best feedback I received from her was the red markings on my graded papers. When I challenged her thinking in class, she degraded me in front of my peers. In fact, the only meaningful conversation that she ever had with me took place just two days before I graduated from high school. At the end of the period, she asked to speak with me alone at the back of the classroom. I thought to myself, "Finally, after four years she's going to apologize." I could not have been more wrong.

As I stood in her back office, she spoke words that to this day are ingrained in my memory. She said, "Damen, I want to tell you something that I have been wanting to say for four years now. I question your potential because I think all you are is just a big weenie."

Looking back, I'm surprised at her choice of the word "weenie" when she had so many other demeaning words to choose from, but nevertheless I understood her message. Not surprised at all by the feelings that she shared, I said, "Ms. Leystan, if I cared a bit about what you thought about me, I would be really disappointed, but the fact is I don't."

What hurt me as I left that classroom was not that she didn't like me, nor that she didn't believe in me. As you have read, I had parents who took on that role and supported me plenty. What saddened me was the fact that if she had had such a conversation with me, I could only imagine how many other students she had talked to in the same way.

Ms. Leystan's behavior was and is representative of a person who completely lost sight of her purpose as a teacher. I believed then, as I do now, that she entered the profession with the best of intentions just like 99.9% of the educators who do across the country. Her flaw, however, was not just that she lost sight of the real work of teaching, but more so that her colleagues and the school did as well. They never joined together in any way, shape, or form to endorse a model of promoting an educational experience that would enhance the lives of students. In fact, they never even decided exactly what they stood for as a school. Every teacher worked privately with a level of independent thinking that exuded an aura of selfishness that would make Paris Hilton look like Mother Teresa. In turn, this selfishness put students into a cycle of academic and social failure that continued for many years to come. The word *sad* does not even begin to accurately describe this kind of culture. What is the best defense of such a culture? How do we ensure that we don't lose sight of the commitments that we all made as inspired new educators entering the profession? We pledge our commitments to each other through a comprehensive endorsement of best practices.

The NEU Endorsement

The NEU endorsement was purposefully created with simplicity in mind. It is the result of a staff's work on the exceptional systems, commitments, schedules, and strategies that have been developed to promote school-wide success. Never a byproduct of any kind of mandate from the top down, this endorsement is genuine, practical, and referred to often as a guide to support student learning for all. Every documented system within the endorsement includes the strategies, commitments, and schedules that play a part in promoting the kind of unity that instills accountability from one classroom to the next. This endorsement, which is seen in its entirety in Appendix A, is representative of the collective work of a staff's ideas.

It is crucial that staff play a major role in the development of an endorsement and the systems within it. When a principal creates systems, they will remain in place for as long as that principal continues as the leader of the school. However, when created by a staff with the guidance of a principal, these systems will remain far beyond the tenure of their leader. And because of the constant state of flux in which administrators often find themselves, we are better served to develop our endorsements with this in mind.

Endorsements can contain anything that is deemed to be critical to the success of a school. NEU endorsements go beyond most by including agreed-upon plans to promote college readiness on site. While there is no checklist for the specific items that must be included, each endorsement should have the following components:

1. *Documentation of your school's pledge:* Some schools

refer to this as a mission or purpose statement, while others call it a school-wide promise. What you call it is not important in the least. What is important is whether the words can be recalled and, more importantly, lived by a school's stakeholders. I have worked with many schools that spent hundreds of man-hours developing statements that were a mile long and an inch deep. The result of their work may have ended up in a frame or on a poster that is strategically hung on the wall in the front office, but more often than not they were too long for anyone to recall, much less act upon.

Many schools write statements like these either because they have to or because they think it's just something that they are supposed to do. It's time for all of us to say what we mean and live by what we say. And because I have yet to meet an educator who can reflect, recite, or even remember a 100-word mission statement as they teach, let's try to keep our words simple and to the point. The 18-word pledge of Los Pen has always been something that is at the top of every important document produced by our school. From letters to parents, to staff meeting agendas, the words *"We are committed to creating a school that knows no limits to the academic success of each student"* are a preamble of sorts that precede any message that we wish to send. These words, which are used by many NEU schools as well as other, non-NEU schools, describe our deep desire to find the potential in all of our students and prepare them for the future.

2. *Explanation of your school's one goal:* I have seen the results when schools set out to create goals for everything under the sun. I have met educators who had so many goals that they could not recall a single one of them. Definitions for goals are numerous, but I personally enjoy the definition of a goal as "the object of a person's ambition." The word "object" is both singular and targeted. Because of this, I don't believe in schools having more than one goal. Of course there may be numerous things that a school needs to work on, but in my opinion, I don't think this automatically warrants the creation of additional goals. Rather, I would suggest that we seek not to make more goals but instead to develop different strategies to meet our school's top goal. Our one goal is simple: *Every student, without exception and without excuse, will be proficient or advanced in reading, writing, and math.* Everything else that others may describe as a goal is really just a strategy to help us achieve our one goal.

Remember, depending on your level, your one goal may very well be different than the one that I have described. This is because the priorities of every school are very diverse, especially when comparing the needs of elementary schools to that of secondary schools. In the end, your staff must decide what is most important to the success of your students and create one goal to follow as you move forward.

3. ***Systems and commitments that promote unity:*** Every system and commitment that a school has documented must be in an NEU endorsement. Some examples within our endorsement are the collaboration commitment, the assessment plan, student goals, the primary intervention model, the code of conduct, and many agreements in regard to the strategies that will be implemented as a part of a No Excuses University.

4. ***Schedules:*** Schedules are nothing if not abundant in schools. Because of this, NEU endorsements should include every important schedule that a teacher needs to refer to throughout the year.

5. ***Accessibility:*** Every NEU endorsement must be accessible. At the end of each school year, our school's leadership team finalizes all of the components within our endorsement and then forwards the entire document to teams for review. In an effort to both save paper and create appropriate access, the endorsement is never placed in a master file or binder; rather, it is developed into a PDF document that is placed on the desktop of every computer in the school. Staff members refer to the document often to guide them in planning throughout the school year.

6. ***Signatures:*** Finally, every NEU endorsement is signed by each member of the staff. This is not contractual in nature. It is a promise to support the content within the endorsement that comes from the heart. If someone

chooses not to sign, that is absolutely his or her choice. What most schools find, however, is that 100% of a staff takes pride in the work represented in an endorsement and eagerly signs this last page, which is framed and placed in a prominent area of the school. This is because the work is representative of their plans and strategies, not ideas that have been given to them.

The act of having an endorsement in writing is so important because it grounds us as a staff. NEU endorsements make note of what we stand for and act as visual reminders of the commitments that we have made to our colleagues next door or across the campus. Endorsements are meant to be more than words on paper; they are expressions of the ideals that have the potential to turn our schools into great academic organizations. They help us capture our beliefs on a daily basis and guard us from the trap of falling into the habits of teachers like Ms. Leystan and her colleagues. As I reflect back on the sad nature of her attitude, I must confess that I did find one source of tremendous joy after I left her room every day. That joy had nothing to do with being liberated from the desk within her classroom and everything to do with seeing the smiling faces of hundreds of elementary school children.

When I became a sophomore, my former elementary school principal, Kevin Ogden, created a special arrangement with my high school principal to allow me to work as a yard duty for second- and third-graders at Julian Elementary as part of an elective class. I will never forget my first day with those kids. The moment my foot hit that blacktop, it was the defining moment of my life. I knew right then and there that I wanted to spend the rest of my life working to support elementary school children. Twenty-five years later, the significance of that day has never worn off. I believe that such an experience is not unique to me. In fact, most of the educators whom I have met can easily recall their moment as well. The key, however, to maintaining a passion for our work is not whether or not we can recall such moments, but whether those moments drive us on a daily basis. Because experiences like these represent the times in our lives when we were most passionate about our profession, we must maintain a personal commitment to recapturing that passion every day. Doing so reminds us of our need to fight the kind of selfishness that sometimes pollutes our profession, and to act as stewards for our students' success.

CHAPTER TWELVE

Theory to Practice

Items for Articulation

❏ In order for a staff to unify around one endorsement, they must first build relationships based on respect and professionalism. Which areas of strength can your staff build upon in these two areas? What areas of challenge still exist and how might you work to address them?

Items for Action

❏ One of the most valuable activities a school can participate in is the creation of a document like the NEU endorsement. As found in Appendix A, the sample endorsement includes all of the systems and schedules that are used to unify a school's commitment to students. As a school, begin the work of creating your own endorsement. Your goal should be to improve your endorsement each year so as to become more explicit in your unified work as a staff.

Endorsements should be worked on during the last few months of each school year, as opposed to the first few months when school begins. Such proactive planning will allow your staff to come back to school from summer vacation having schedules and systems in place and knowing exactly what they stand for as a school community.

KEY CONCEPTS

"Build for your team a feeling of oneness, of dependence on one another, and of strength to be derived by unity."

— Vince Lombardi

1 There is a big difference between schools that promote college readiness and No Excuses Universities.

2 Schools must apply for No Excuses University status before they can use the trademarked name and logo.

3 Not every school that applies is granted NEU status.

4 Every school within the NEU Network of Schools must communicate, collaborate, and show continuous improvement in order to remain in the network.

JOINING THE NO EXCUSES UNIVERSITY NETWORK OF SCHOOLS

In January 2004, a small southern California elementary school became a source of inspiration by creating a college readiness initiative known as the No Excuses University. In just a few short years, that inspiration has motivated educators and schools across the country to take a similar path. As of June 2009, there were 62 official No Excuses Universities in ten states across America. The thousands of educators at these very diverse schools (K-5, K-6, K-8, middle, junior high, and charter) collectively support more than 35,000 students, many living in challenging environments where poverty is the standard. No Excuses University staff members understand that we are in a race against the clock where the stakes could not be higher. (See how our network

189

is growing by visiting www.turnaroundschools.com.)

There's a difference between schools that promote college readiness and schools that are officially accepted into the No Excuses University Network. Because of this, we take great lengths to protect the integrity of this model. Everything that you have read in this book about promoting college readiness can be done within your classroom and your school with two exceptions. Only schools that have been recognized as official NEU campuses are allowed to use the trademarked No Excuses University name and logo associated with this endeavor. While the rewards of being a part of this movement are great, the expectations for the schools that are accepted are extremely high.

The act of being granted official No Excuses University status should not be looked at as an award. Participating as a No Excuses University is so much more than that. It is a way of life. Schools are not asked to pay a membership fee, nor are they required to pay dues of any kind. The purpose of creating a network like ours is to connect like-minded educators with a passion to learn from one another, work collaboratively, and participate in an educational reform effort that has the potential to change the face of public education as we know it.

As the founder of this endeavor, I take this responsibility very seriously. Schools that wish to join the network must participate in an application process that is reviewed by a committee of NEU educators and supporters. Not every school that applies is allowed into the NEU Network. In fact, not every school that has been accepted as an official No Excuses University is allowed to remain in the network. A yearly re-application process takes place, as schools are held accountable for continuous growth in the development and implementation of exceptional systems that focus on promoting college readiness for all. Finally, schools are also judged on their collaborative contributions to the network. Schools who wish to join must continually ask themselves, "What value do we *add* to the No Excuses University Network of Schools?"

Joining the Network

Schools seeking membership into the No Excuses University Network can participate in the application process after attending a TurnAround Schools conference with a team that has to include the principal. It is imperative that each team, including the principal, represent all grade levels or departments. After attending a conference, schools apply through a written submission that focuses on seven specific questions about the implementation of the six TurnAround Schools exceptional systems, as well as a video submission that displays a school's college readiness commitment at work. A committee, which selects only schools that show extraordinary passion and drive for the NEU model, reviews each application. This application, which can be seen in Appendix B, guides interested parties through the process. The guidance for a successful application is vague for a reason. Our desire is to select schools that are already displaying the ideals of the NEU model, not schools that have written to a rubric to receive a specific score.

Entrance into the No Excuses University Network is granted to schools on a year-to-year basis. Each year, schools take part in a short re-application process to give evidence of the growth that they have made from one year to the next. Schools that do not continue to meet the declared expectations or who show a lack of desire to make improvements are dropped as official NEU schools.

Our ambition is to be associated with the best and brightest in our profession, but this does not mean that we seek to be an elitist organization. Many of our schools are far from being the top-performing in their district. In fact, some of our schools are challenged by a looming status of *program improvement* that makes others wary of forming long-term partnerships. We are different. We initially select schools based on potential, and retain them as official members based on performance. This endeavor can be successful at any school that is willing to participate in innovative practices that promote college readiness. The most successful schools are the ones that step out unafraid as they eagerly seek to meet the expectations placed on every official No Excuses University.

Expectations of NEU Schools

Far more important for a school than being accepted into the network is its ability to meet the day-to-day expectations that come with being an official NEU school. We have observed several schools that made the mistake of thinking that their No Excuses University status was some kind of an award. They thought that their work was over after the application process. In reality, that's when the work really begins.

The No Excuses University Network is not for everyone. Both the organization and I have no desire to partner with educators who do not share the same core values that we do. Even though every NEU principal must sign an agreement that carefully describes the expectations of participating schools, there have been several who, frankly, just don't get it. Because of this, many schools have been asked to leave the network as quickly as they were asked to join. In the spirit of learning from their mistakes, let me clearly lay out the expectations of a No Excuses University school should you be interested in joining us in this endeavor. They can easily be remembered as the "Three C's."

COMMUNICATION

Recently, I called to talk to the principal of a school within our network. For several months, I had observed an absence in communication between the school and our organization, which prompted some concern on my part. I spoke to the secretary: "Good morning. My name is Damen Lopez and I am the founder of the No Excuses University. May I speak with your principal?"

Her response was, "What is the No Excuses University?"

Let's just say this didn't exactly alleviate my concerns. This secretary's lack of understanding about the NEU endeavor was a reflection of the lackluster communication that had been taking place. It was clear that this school viewed their acceptance as a one-time activity that gave them permission to use what many see as a memorable name and catchy logo. After a very candid conversation with the principal, I let them know that this was not the case.

Members of the NEU Foundation, our non-profit organization that supports the network, or I, contact No Excuses University schools on a monthly basis. These communications typically take place via email or over the phone and are used to update principals about the status of our work. Exciting news about sister schools, important information about upcoming events, or inquiries requiring feedback are the most common reasons for our communications. We ask all NEU principals to respond to this information as well as share the great things happening in their buildings. As each year brings staffing modifications, it is the principal's duty to share any changes that take place, especially when it comes to site leadership. When a principal is transferred, resigns, or retires, it is imperative that the school contacts our organization in a timely manner. This enables us to offer support for the new leader and keep the momentum moving forward. New principals are required to attend a TurnAround Schools Institute as well. The role that No Excuses University principals play is significant. They are the voice and face of their campus. Their excitement, or lack thereof, for this endeavor is a reflection of the entire staff. They are the link between their site and our organization. Out of all the expectations that we have for No Excuses University schools, the responsibility of a principal to model effective communication is at the top of the list.

COLLABORATION

Bringing together educators from around the country is a challenge that is often limited by geography. In today's Internet age, however, we have been able to minimize this challenge by creating a web portal for all No Excuses University staff members. Members can log in and view message board comments, participate in blog discussions, search for like-minded colleagues who share the same grade or university partnership, and exchange lesson plan ideas via email. The potential for this form of collaboration is tremendous. As our ability to offer tools for our staff members to collaborate increases, the expectations for each of them to participate will grow as well. There is so much that we can learn from one another that will further our cause and continue to change the lives of our students.

In addition to the online collaborative format that we have created for teachers and staff, TurnAround Schools holds an NEU Principal's Retreat each year. With an atmosphere of friendly fellowship that bonds us, these retreats are used as a time for each principal to present effective ideas face to face with one another. All principals are encouraged to participate. A similar format will be developed for teachers and other staff members as part of a National No Excuses University Convention that will take place every year beginning in 2011.

CONTINUOUS IMPROVEMENT

Finally, No Excuses University schools are expected to show continuous improvement for their students, both academically and socially. As part of the yearly re-application process, schools are never compared to others within the network, but instead to the results that they themselves have earned from one year to the next. This kind of comparison allows us to ensure that the work behind the "window dressing" is taking place and the focus on academic results remains prominent.

NO EXCUSES UNIVERSITY TESTIMONIALS

As you can see, this endeavor is only for the most bold and passionate among us. Most schools do not typically seek the expectations that we place on those within the network. However, because of their desire to step away from the status quo, No Excuses Universities are realizing results that are exciting their entire school communities. After reading what some of our principals have said about their participation in the No Excuses University movement, I think you'll find that they would have it no other way.

In the two years that Lake Louise Elementary School in Palatine has been a member of the No Excuses University Network, our partnership has had a significantly positive  *impact on parents, staff, and most importantly, students. I have been honored to witness and learn about numerous inspirational anecdotes demonstrating the power of college readiness on elementary children. During the 2008–2009 school year, our Student Council, lead by Ms. Beth DeAnda, created a college scholarship presented to a former Lake Louise student. In the scholarship's first year, our students raised $500. Upon reviewing many applications from former Lake Louise students, the Student Council and staff were able to award the scholarship to a very deserving graduate and will be helping her realize her dream of becoming a college graduate. Through experiencing this process, the students at Lake Louise have witnessed that their dream of being a college graduate is possible, no excuses!*

Adam Palmer
Principal
Lake Louise Elementary
Palatine, IL

Becoming a No Excuses University has brought the staff of Lowrie Elementary together to celebrate successes and plan together for challenges. Reflecting on our experience, the most powerful aspect so far has been the camaraderie that shared accountability has provided us. To begin with, a handful of teachers attended a workshop and returned to share their unbridled enthusiasm with colleagues. Next, we moved forward, as the staff attended training together and came to the realization that we certainly do have something special happening at our school! Documenting the exceptional systems that make Lowrie a special place to learn gave everyone a chance to dream big. Recording our application video gave us a glimpse into the excitement that our students hold about their futures. Finally, celebrating

collaboratively with our students when we were accepted as a No Excuses University on May 25, 2009 made us realize our journey is just beginning.

Kelly O'Brien
Principal
Lowrie Elementary
Elgin, IL

No Excuses University served as a stimulus for teachers to unite for a common goal—to make sure every student meets or exceeds grade-level standards in reading, writing, and mathematics. NEU encouraged us to identify systems we had in place and provided an umbrella for coordinating our efforts towards refining and expanding those systems to make them exceptional. This model sent a message to our children that anything is possible even though they come from a low socioeconomic area. NEU is truly making a difference in the lives of our children.

Cheri Gibson
Principal
Don Pedro Elementary
Ceres, CA

I walked into my office one day to see a small piece of stationery on my desk. It had been one of those months where the walls were caving in and the hours seemed to get longer each day. I wondered if what I was doing, what my staff was doing, would impact my student body. I looked down at my desk and saw these words written by one of my struggling first-grade students: "We can go to college because we have NO excuses." Does No Excuses work? It does for that one first-grade student, and that one makes everything worth it.

Faith Rivera
Principal
Virginia Lake Elementary
Palatine, IL

The power of the No Excuses University experience is far reaching and brings opportunities to teachers, school staff, parents, students, and the community that were not present before. Prior to our school's dedication to the No Excuses ideology, our school's sense of collaboration and community were weak. Over the past three years as a No Excuses school, the growth and progress our school has made for students and families is priceless. The commitment teachers, staff, families, and students have made to excellence and high quality education will last our students a lifetime. During this period of growth, we have added a Heritage Wall to the center of our school, which showcases various tiles made by families at our school. As part of the partnership with

200

parents and families, we were also fortunate enough to take students and their family members on a field trip to USC this past year. The experience and journey of No Excuses has shown teachers and school staff the ways to get students to succeed and how the greatness of a school truly does come from within.

Lucy Medina
Principal
Agua Caliente Elementary
Palm Springs, CA

The No Excuses University philosophy has created a paradigm shift at Kenyon Woods. The university focus has given relevance in the eyes of the students to the assessments they are required to take. They are not only excited about the prospect of going to college, but feel empowered to take control of their education. MAP scores are no longer just numbers; they are indicators to the students of what areas they need to strengthen in order to reach their goal of a higher education. As we integrate our existing programs into NEU and develop new exceptional systems where they are needed, support for both students and staff is strengthened. This framework, combined with focused leadership and boundless enthusiasm has created our "culture of universal achievement," which is felt throughout the building. Our *daily morning mantra "We are Kenyon Woods, and we dream big!" is more than just a saying; it's a philosophy our entire building works to embody.*

Sue Welu
Principal
Kenyon Woods Middle
Elgin, IL

The NEU model has kept our school moving towards the ultimate goal of academic achievement for all students regardless of the immense challenges we may face. Our students now know what year they will graduate from college and what it will take to get them there. They are proud to be part of a school that believes that they too deserve the opportunity to be educated in a way that prepares them for college. Becoming a No Excuses University school has helped to decrease suspension and retention rates, while increasing attendance and academic performance. Mango Elementary is proud to be a member of the No Excuses University family.

Sara Najarro-Kurland
Principal
Mango Elementary
Fontana, CA

A *little kindergarten boy at our school walked up to his teacher's desk with the question, "Can I borrow your stapler?" The teacher responded by handing the stapler to the boy, who immediately tried, without success, to cram it into his pockets, which were already bulging with pencils, erasers, and other school supplies. As he waddled back toward his desk, he was asked by his teacher, "What are you going to do with all that stuff in your pockets?" His answer was instant, and far-reaching. "I'm going to college, Mrs. Burrell." The power of No Excuses University is the undeterred, genuine hope it creates in the life of a child. The gift of No Excuses University is that it is not*

concerned with where a child comes from; it is focused only on where they are going.

Burke Staheli
Principal
Washington Elementary
Washington, UT

Vermont Elementary School in San Bernardino, California has 750 students on a multi-track year-round system where the majority of our students come from poverty and are English Language Learners. We recognize the power of an effective partnership with our parents and community. To that end, we have developed Vermont Parent University as the vehicle to create that partnership and, ultimately, dramatically increase our academic achievement. Our parents are our partners in education and they have been an untapped resource. In 2009, our inaugural year of Vermont Parent University, we graduated 120 parents. As the only No Excuses University school in San Bernardino County, our goal is that the Vermont Elementary School community will develop a "no excuses" attitude toward education and achieve uncommon results from this rural, distressed area.

Elizabeth Atkinson
Principal
Vermont Elementary
San Bernardino, CA

At Jane Addams Elementary School we have embraced
the No Excuses University philosophy and program. In
our first year of implementation, we have seen students
and parents responding to the importance and need for our
students to know that college is an expectation and not just
a dream. With a diverse population, No Excuses University
has given our students a light at the end of the tunnel. From
pep assemblies to university pen pals, to college speakers,
high school speakers, community members from different
occupations, to even our own mascot, our first year was
a huge success. Throughout the school year, parents and
students have used the motto of "No Excuses" to teachers
and administration when it came to obstacles put in their
path. Teachers have embraced the message and standards
have never been higher for our kids. This program has
transformed Jane Addams into a school that has a sense of

community and most importantly family. On Fridays we wear our No Excuses shirts and parents and community members are amazed at the sea of blue and white on the playground and in the halls. The notion and belief that all students will be college ready has been a message that our staff has sent to our kids from the first day of school. This is a wonderful network and at Jane Addams we are honored to be a part of a truly magnificent program.

David Morris
Principal
Jane Addams
Palatine, IL

No Excuses University has given our school structure for all the beliefs we have about our students. Using this structure to motivate our students towards excellence has made a measurable difference. The vocabulary is just a jumping-off point for our students. Fifth-grade students would ask at what age they could quit school. Now they are planning on where they will go to college! More of our parents are also going to college and thinking about the opportunities they could have with a post-high school education. NEU gives our students opportunities they never knew they had!

Cheryl Dixon
Teacher
Moffitt Elementary
Springfield, OR

I have been blessed and honored to become the principal of Los Peñasquitos Elementary School following Damen Lopez and Jeff King, former co-principals. I can personally attest to the uniqueness of this revelation. I am often asked what is at the foundation of this amazing elementary school and I easily reply, "The staff." At the heart of this extraordinary experience is an exemplary staff that breathes passion for student success. The common core belief is that collectively we are responsible and accountable for student success and achievement. This group constantly implements strategies to set aside the "baggage" children often bring with them, allowing instruction to reach students. If a child does not respond, they look to adjust instruction with a never-give-up attitude. They continually set high expectations for themselves and our students. The exceptional systems serve as a framework for excellence, providing a clear direction and momentum of this unique culture. This recipe for success withstands the transition of personnel. A climate exists where commitment to excellence grows and the staff works to inspire, motivate, and nurture individuals to exceed their potential. WELCOME TO NEU!!

Deanne McLaughlin
Principal
Los Peñasquitos Elementary
San Diego, CA

Each year in May there is an Immigration Rally in Chicago. Hispanic families sometimes take their children out of school to attend. Aylin, a fifth-grade student in Mrs.

Schneiss's class at Lincoln School in Palatine, planned to attend the rally with her father. Once they got to Chicago, she convinced her father to instead spend time at Northwestern University, where she wants to attend someday. Aylin's father was happy to oblige and they had a wonderful time on their very own college visit.

Mary Beth Knoeppel
Assistant Principal
Lincoln Elementary
Palatine, IL

As part of the Gray M. Sanborn No Excuses University program, students in grades 1-6 had the opportunity to take a field trip to Northwestern University in Evanston, Illinois in May of 2009. This trip allowed our students to visit the campus and tour facilities that included student athletics, academic services, the Welsh-Ryan Arena, Ryan Field, and Rocky Miller Park. Northwestern student athletes met with Sanborn students and shared their college experiences, challenges, and accomplishments. Head football coach Pat Fitzgerald met all 600 Sanborn guests and provided a pep talk about academic responsibilities. This is just one example of the kinds of experiences that Sanborn students have received as a result of our college readiness focus.

Michael Carmody
Principal
Sanborn Elementary
Palatine, IL

The No Excuses University at Harvest Valley is an exceptional school within an exceptional network of schools. Each student has at least two individual academic goals, which are formed at our fall and winter Goal Setting Breakfasts with the students, parents, and teachers. As the students meet their individual goals, they are placed on the "I Met My Goal" wall of fame. During the 2008–2009 school year, 96% of the students met their individual goals. We work as one community of students, parents, teachers, and

210

administrators to achieve our mission statement of becoming a distinguished school filled with proficient college-bound students. We show our strong belief in our students through our actions and our surroundings. Each classroom has been adopted by a four-year university and proudly hangs the flag outside their door. We have positive affirmations and murals throughout the school to remind the students daily of their dedication to excellence. At Harvest Valley we truly believe and act upon our belief that all students can and will succeed!

Michelle Rodriguez
Principal
Harvest Valley Elementary
Romoland, CA

211

No Excuses University inspired me to establish a pen pal program with Illinois State University for my intermediate classroom of students with emotional disabilities. The assistant women's athletic director was incredibly supportive as she recruited the perfect mix of college students who became positive role models for my class. After our class earned 1,000 Reggie (ISU mascot) grams for displaying positive behavior, our pen pals took it upon themselves to travel three hours to make a surprise visit with Reggie in tow. The bond between pen pals and students reached beyond pencil and paper. Their connection helped my students *realize the importance of their own goals, both immediate and long term. Now my students can visualize themselves going to college. Many students, parents, and pen pals said they are better for having gone through this experience. As a teacher I couldn't agree more!*

Stephanie Kovarik
3-6 ED Teacher
Whitley Elementary
Hoffman Estates, IL

The concept of No Excuses University is clear and simple. It's something that school faculty, students, and parents can all grasp and put into action in support of improving not only the experiences of our students while they're with us, but more importantly, the lives they lead once they've moved on. At Devonshire School in Skokie, Illinois, we believe deeply in the ideals that No Excuses stands for in supporting our students and facilitating and leading their progress and growth. The exceptional systems we have instilled around professional collaboration and data-based decision making are going to make a difference in the lives of our students. They're going to college. They know it. We know it and we're all proud to be a part of this exceptional school community.

Randy Needlman
Principal
Devonshire Elementary
Skokie, IL

At Willow Bend the culmination of our No Excuses Program was a Cash for College fundraiser in which we raised money for former Willow Bend students who needed financial assistance for college. During the 2008–2009 school year, more than $2,000 was raised through donating money to wear hats to school, beach wear, favorite sports team apparel, and other various fundraisers. Parents were to encourage their children to do extra chores or take on responsibilities to earn money for this fundraiser. In addition, the Willow Bend staff made child-friendly baskets and sold raffle tickets for the purpose of raising money. Each classroom had a jar to collect donations; the office staff did as well. At the end of the year, we had an assembly to announce the three high school scholarship winners. This was a great way to end the year and involve the surrounding community in the No Excuses program.

Rachel Bland
Assistant Principal
Willow Bend
Rolling Meadows, IL

Since the John Muir Literacy Academy joined the No Excuses network three years ago, the NEU ideology has impacted our school as measured by increased student achievement. More importantly, the NEU way has changed our community's mindset and led to the shared belief that ALL CHILDREN are capable of enhancing their lives through higher education. Our staff instills this belief in *students by teaching our district's essential outcomes, creating meaningful systems, and motivating students through the*

powerful symbolism of college readiness. Muir was considered a "failing" school two years ago when our students with special needs did not make adequate yearly progress (AYP). In 2008 and 2009, Muir showed continuous improvement. This year 11 of our 12 subgroups of students have improved on the Illinois Standards Achievement Test; all subgroups have met or exceeded state standards; and students posted the highest scores ever at Muir School.

Brad Carter
Principal
John Muir Literacy Academy
Hoffman Estates, IL

We have developed a Culture of Universal Achievement at Dove Academy that challenges our students, staff, and parents to look beyond an elementary school, middle school, or even high school education. Our No Excuses University Program is driving the evolution of our school from a good academy to a great one. As a charter school, we are a school of choice. Our funding is based upon our enrollment. For our school to exist, *we have to distinguish ourselves from the variety of educational programs offered in the metro Detroit area. We have to give the families in our community a reason to select our academy as their elementary school. The development of our No Excuses University Program has furthered our efforts to become a school of substance. We are becoming a school of "first choice" for our community. The results from our efforts this school year are pouring in. We cut our grade level retentions in half and on average we beat the Detroit public schools on every state test that we administer. More than 96% of our students re-enrolled for next school year and we surpassed every Adequate Yearly Progress (AYP) Target that we had to meet. This year, Dove Academy was recognized by the Michigan Department of Education for Beating the Odds, achieving 80% proficiency on the state math test and nearly 70% proficiency in English Language Arts — even though nearly 60% of our students are "economically disadvantaged." Working with Damen and developing our No Excuses University Program has helped us realize that for our students to prepare happy and successful lives, they need to learn about college now. All of our students will be proficient in reading, writing, and math. All of our students must build their character. Our students are college bound and they know it!*

Frank Nardelli
Principal
Dove Academy K-7
Detroit, MI

No Excuses University has had more of an impact at Winchester Elementary School than anyone could have foretold. The bond many of our classes have formed with university/college organizations, including athletics and alumni, has our students excited for the opportunities that lie ahead of them after high school. Students who previously had no thought of attending a university/college have now begun preparing to attend by opening a savings account or looking at options to pay for tuition through partnerships with a local bank and credit union. Many of our parents are excited that their child will be the first in their family to attend college. Our school has started a college scholarship fund for Winchester Elementary "Alumni" to help one child each year pay part of *his or her tuition. It's hard to believe any of this would have happened if not for the No Excuses University philosophy.*

Mark Delano
Principal
Winchester Elementary
Hemet, CA

Kenda Parkey, a kindergarten teacher, was having her students participate in math centers. One of the centers for the day was free choice with math manipulatives. Kenda was instructing her math lesson at the back table with a group. During her lesson, she could hear the words "college," "teaching," and "going to school" coming from another center. When the bell rang to change centers, she went to the manipulative center and noticed an amazing arrangement on the carpet and asked her students what it was. Her students told her the kangaroos were all going to college and the bears were teaching them. The group insisted on leaving their college up for the next group. Each group continued to add more to the "college." Wow. It is amazing, when you open up the world to children, what five-year-olds can see! No Excuses University really is awakening hope, determination, and persistence in all of the students at Prince Elementary School.

Tassi Call
Principal
Prince Elementary
Tucson, AZ

"No Excuses" and "University" are the keys to success in relation to Landau School's goals as a professional learning community and as a member of the NEU network. Damen's presentation to all teachers on a staff development day was the catalyst for a deepened commitment to each student by all staff members. The excitement about the NEU concept can be captured in many ways: students' pride in wearing a university t-shirt; an overheard statement, "I want to be in that classroom next year, because that's my favorite university"; students chanting "No excuses, no siree, no excuses, not for me!"; teachers having collaborative discussions about common assessment results and the effectiveness of teaching strategies, and the next steps for those students who did not succeed; 90 students with perfect attendance for the school year; and seeing *the intervention system work as students exit the program to reenter reading instruction in their own classrooms!*

Lynne Keating
Principal
Landau Elementary
Cathedral City, CA
San Diego, CA

Our vision: College readiness for all students. No excuses! To that end, we strategically set and work towards specific goals. School goals, teacher goals, class goals, and student goals illuminate our direction. The Jane Stenson faculty collaboratively and systematically uses staff development time to evaluate student data for school growth and individual progress. Instructional decision-making is directly linked to this data. We rally for our students by providing multiple-leveled interventions. We work with our families and our community as we champion student learning. College readiness is a mindset, a mantra, a driving force. We have brought our students to colleges and we have brought colleges to our students. From the college t-shirts and university banners to the student-generated College Fair and the beautiful ceramic mural depicting our path to college, the expectations are clear. Jane Stenson students will be college ready and college minded!

Sue O'Neill
Principal
Jane Stenson Elementary
Skokie, IL

My second-grade bilingual teacher called me to her classroom to see what one of her students was wearing. I was thinking—what it could be? She brought me one of her students, who is a second language learner and a struggling student. I saw that she was wearing a Texas Tech lanyard. I asked the child why she was wearing it, thinking that she would tell me that it was because her teacher went to school there. She told me that her father bought it for her because this was where she was going to go to college. When she goes to college, she will be the first in her family to attend college.

Haidi Appel
Principal
Mitzi Bond Elementary
El Paso, TX

On Sunday, June 14th we had our first Eighth Grade Closing Exercises and Farewell Ceremony. This was the first class to leave First Philadelphia on their journey to high school. The students sought admission to many renowned high schools in the Philadelphia area over this past year, and our departing students will be attending 20 different fabulous high schools next year. No Excuses helped our eighth-grade students to stay focused on achieving at high levels during their final year at First Philadelphia. The majority of students received proficient or advanced on the state's standardized testing. Student success crossed all ethnic and economic backgrounds. At our final ceremony, the students individually addressed the audience to announce where they would be *going to high school, their favorite memory at First Philly, and one of their goals for the future. Every student stood before the entire faculty and his/her parents to declare that s/he would be going to college. Thank you No Excuses!*

Kristine Magargee
Principal
First Philadelphia Charter School
of Literacy
Philadelphia, PA

Every morning for the last two years, all Killybrooke students have started the day with the cheer "Killybrooke is college bound!" shouted three times. We believe that every student is able to meet or exceed grade-level standards and that we can begin in elementary school to prepare all of them for college. Our goal is made clear in everything we do. Our commitment to preparing students for college has resulted in phenomenal academic success for our students, particularly our "at-promise" students. We are very proud to be a California Distinguished and Title 1 Academic Achievement Award School. We enthusiastically join the other No Excuses Universities across the country in preparing our students for a fulfilling future by preparing them for college!

Kathy Sanchez
Principal
Killybrooke Elementary
Costa Mesa, CA

Three years ago, a teacher and I went to the NWEA Conference and heard a keynote by Damen. His presentation hit home and we immediately knew that our belief in ALL students was missing. After sharing NEU with our staff, Hanover Countryside became alive with ideas. From pep rallies to fight songs, college partnerships to community collaborations, Hanover Countryside has become a proud and dedicated member of the NEU Network. Together we know that anything is possible for our students.

Leslie Kleiman
Principal
Hanover Countryside Elementary
Steamwood, IL

Sometimes it's the personal stories that illustrate the power and need of the NEU framework, and Jovanny's story is one of those. Jovanny came to us as an angry and defiant seventh grader. After his second or third trip to my office, we began to talk about his experience in sixth grade. He shared with me that he had been called a "zero" and was a member of the Zero Club, a title and group named by his sixth-grade teachers for students who did not do homework, instead earning zeroes on the work. The effects of this were evident: Jovanny did not trust the adults in school, he was not motivated to change his work habits, and he established adversarial relationships with his teachers. He also admitted to giving in to the temptations and lure of the gang in his neighborhood and spending a lot of time with the members. It took an entire year to gain

Jovanny's trust, but as we worked toward that, we talked about the future. Jovanny's academic potential was evident from the first conversation with him; however, it was not something he or his parents talked about. During a meeting with the family, I asked Jovanny's father what his hopes were for Jovanny. His thoughts were for Jovanny to work on cars because it was good work and could earn him a good salary. I stressed college for Jovanny to him and his wife, explaining the potential in their son and the importance of education. Jovanny's two years in junior high were not easy. Having consistent systems in place across the building allowed him to hear consistent messages and have consistent expectations with each of his teachers. By the second semester of eighth grade, Jovanny understood the need for education in order to have the future he wanted. He talked about attending Ohio State, having learned about their soccer program. We connected him with the soccer coach at the high school, who came and met with him to establish a relationship and share the expectations for playing on a team at the high school level.

Jovanny earned Honor Roll status his last two quarters of junior high, and his pride in his achievements was evident in the smile that had replaced the anger and defiance. He is on his way to the future he deserves.

Mary Baum
Principal
Winston Campus Junior High
Palatine, IL

As I reflect on this year there have been great accomplishments and others still to conquer. We began with attending the TurnAround Schools NEU retreat two years ago and I was eager to jump on board. However, I knew we had work to do at Rosemary Kennedy Elementary in order to receive the honor of truly becoming an NEU school. Many of my teachers wondered why we were moving slowly and why we didn't order shirts for everyone because it was such a great concept. Today I had a conversation with someone and shared with them that now we had earned the privilege of wearing the NEU logo. This has been a great beginning to our journey. The concept of NEU infused energy needed to move forward and not just face challenges but overcome them. We have implemented School-wide Intervention for all students and this has yielded great benefits in many different aspects because we are all *responsible for our students' academic gains. The year closed out with grade levels having conversations about students and honesty to be forward with concerns as well as accountability to each other. Often accountability is thought of as a "district concept." Today at RMK, it is our job to not just teach our children but ensure that if something isn't happening we will have the conversation as to why and how can we make it happen. I am pleased to say that we are all in make-it-happen mode, which is key to success, and look forward to the new chapter of success we will write in the upcoming school year.*

Jackie Casillas
Principal
Rosemary Kennedy Elementary
Riverside, CA

Four years ago, Anne Fox Elementary School in Hanover Park, Illinois became the first NEU outside of the state of California. The school for years had languished as the lowest achieving school in its district with the percentage of students meeting or exceeding state academic standards on all tests combined at 62% in 2005. Fox School features an extremely diverse student population with a low-income rate of 30%. In spite of demographic challenges, the staff made a collective commitment to become a top-achieving elementary school and placed concerted emphasis on building a culture of universal achievement and refining academic systems to support the learning of all students. Using Los Peñasquitos as a model of best practice and inspiration, Fox's teachers truly came together

227

to clarify the school's mission, form collaborative relationships, assume shared responsibility for student learning and utilize powerful intervention structures to improve academic achievement across the board. In addition, the faculty worked tirelessly to embed the belief that ALL students attending Fox School are college bound and have done this through the use of powerful symbolism and by establishing strong relationships with partnering universities.

In 2009, Fox School received state assessment data and the results were dramatic. Today, more than 95% of Fox's students are meeting state academic standards in all subjects tests (93% in reading and 96% in math). This marks the second consecutive year that Fox School has enjoyed 90/90 status with more than 90% of Fox students meeting state standards in reading and math. These gains in academic achievement could not have materialized without staff members buying in to powerful belief systems in the potential of ALL students and taking it upon themselves to refine systems of support to ensure student success.

Nick Myers
Principal
Anne Fox Elementary
Schaumburg, IL

During the 2007–2008 school year, Winston Campus Elementary was in the early stages of No Excuses University. Our teachers were trying everything to establish a connection with colleges. Our grades 3/4 gifted teacher, Jeanne Grelck, sent

228

out an email to the alumni association at Boston College and received a strange reply. The reply was from Brian Cummins, a lieutenant in the U.S. Army stationed in Iraq and a BC alumni. He was very curious about NEU and he just loved the philosophy. One of Lieutenant Cummins's responsibilities in Iraq was to help rebuild Iraqi schools. In the Iraqi village where he was stationed, Al Qaeda burned down the main school because they consider school "evil." Lieutenant Cummins sent Jeanne's classroom an email including a picture of a third-grade Iraqi classroom. In his email, Lieutenant Cummins described an Iraqi classroom and he explained how lucky U.S. students are to have the opportunity of a public education. Lieutenant Cummins wrote in his email, "When a person is denied an education they are made into a slave. What can one do without an education?" Jeanne's students thought about this and decided to do a service project to help the Iraqi children. On their own, Jeanne's students conducted a toy drive. They worked for weeks collecting toys to give holiday gifts to the Iraqi children. Jeanne's students collected more than 300 toys and sent them to Lieutenant Cummins right before the holidays. Lieutenant Cummins wrote back thanking the students and asking them not to take their education for granted. Jeanne did adopt Boston College and they have had a strong relationship ever since.

Andy Tieman
Principal
Winston Campus Elementary
Palatine, IL

Every morning we start our day with a loud and thunderous, "We are Niños School! We are College Bound!" that resonates throughout the building. Not only do we say these words, we think about the message and most importantly we "believe" in our message. Our students hear our explicit "college bound" message throughout the day and as a result are sharing this message with their families. And they are letting us know that what we are doing is sending a powerful message. At the start of this school year, one of our students' grandparents was compelled to visit our school to share how excited she is that at the elementary level we are talking to our students about college. Another parent celebrates our "No Excuses—College Bound Year" by keeping her co-workers informed about all of our school's "college" efforts. The most compelling story is one shared by a parent, Lisa, and what she had to say about her son's experience in his new school. Andrew has always been a hard child to get interested in and excited about his education. His former schools have been "a struggle" and she felt she could never get him motivated. To her great surprise, from the first day of school, he came home and has talked excitedly and endlessly about how "they talk about all of us going to college, Mom!" He has been sharing everything that happens in his day with her. According to Andrew's mother, "He is enthused, happy, and loves leaving for school every day!" At the end of every school day, our students excitedly exit their classrooms as they walk around the building reciting their college/university *cheer. The cheering is contagious! Our students know that they can "Dream BIG!"*

Dr. Ana Gomez del Castillo
Principal
Kyrene de los Niños Elementary
Tempe, AZ

CHAPTER THIRTEEN
THEORY TO PRACTICE

ITEMS FOR ARTICULATION

❏ In chapter 1, you were encouraged to create a checklist of the reservations that you may have about promoting college readiness to all students and place it inside of an envelope. Take that envelope and open it with your teammates. Which reservations have been alleviated? What challenges or questions still exist for you personally in regard to the promotion of college readiness?

ITEMS FOR ACTION

If you and your colleagues are interested in creating a No Excuses University environment in an effort to join the NEU Network of Schools, consider some of the following suggestions:

❏ Assemble a No Excuses committee to help implement the strategies and ideas necessary for schools to be invited into the NEU Network.

❏ Create a comprehensive plan to promote a spirit of college readiness at your site that is in line with the six exceptional systems found in chapter three.

❏ Take the time to examine Appendix A and B. Many of these items offer tremendous examples for schools to follow.

❏ Review the NEU application found in Appendix B. This will help guide your own journey in discussing the benefits that your school can offer to the network. Schools that apply for official NEU status typically take several months to implement the strategies, ideas, and suggestions offered in this book before submitting their application.

CHAPTER FOURTEEN

EXTRAORDINARY

When I was a new staff member at Los Peñasquitos Elementary, the bell that rang at the end of the day acted as a reminder that the second part of my day was about to begin. Several times a week, I would leave campus around 3:30 p.m. in order to work the 4 p.m. to midnight shift as a bellman at the Radisson Hotel in San Diego. For many months, especially in the summer, the job was filled with meeting interesting people who offered plenty of tips. However, as the years went by and the economy began to dip, the tips went from filling the pockets of my uniform to barely filling the palm of my hand. One night while working alone, I pulled from my pocket three one-dollar bills and lined them in a row on the top of the bell desk. These fruitless symbols of my labor inspired me to make a decision that I had been putting off for several months. I decided right then and there that the job had nothing left to offer me.

As I began to make plans to talk with my boss about resigning, a gentleman summoned me to his car and asked for my assistance with his bags. I loaded my bell cart and proceeded to lead the man to the elevators within the hotel lobby. After delivering the items to his room I said, "Is there anything else I can help you with today, sir?"

Knowing that this was bellman language for, "Could you please tip me?" the man pulled out a crisp five-dollar bill and a brand new copy of a book. Thinking that he was going to give me a book and a five-dollar bill as a bookmark, I was surprised by his offer. He said, "Here's the deal. You can have five bucks or you can have a copy of my brand-new book. But you can't have both."

I knew my answer immediately. I didn't want some book that I knew nothing about. I wanted the five dollars! However, I was raised with enough manners to say to the man, "Sure, I love to read. I'll take the book."

I thanked him and headed downstairs. Exclaiming a few choice words under my breath, I walked to my bell desk with the same amount in my pocket as before, three dollars.

Out of boredom, I sat at the desk and opened up the book that the man gave me. Immediately, I became inspired by the collection of numerous short anecdotes, poems, and writings within the pages. These stories were often about ordinary people who did extraordinary things. I can't say that it was one specific item in the book that made such a profound impact on me, but I do remember being overtaken by a desire to somehow live a life that would influence others. As someone who has always considered himself to be quite ordinary, I finished reading the book feeling like I was very capable of doing something extraordinary. It wasn't until many months later that I realized the gravity of my experiences that afternoon. That man, Jack Canfield, had given me a book, *Chicken Soup for the Soul*, that would later sell more than 80 million copies and inspire people all around the world.

The message that I learned then is as relevant as the message that I try to share today. The No Excuses University Network of Schools is about *ordinary* people coming together to do *extraordinary* things. The strength that is found in the collaborative efforts of one another is immeasurable compared to the limitations of individuals acting alone. I wrote this book knowing that one person can influence a team. A team can influence a school. A school can motivate a collection of like-minded individuals. And, like-minded individuals working together can change the world.

APPENDIX A

NO EXCUSES
UNIVERSITY

NO EXCUSES UNIVERSITY

ENDORSEMENT

NEU Commitment

In 1996, the staff of Los Peñasquitos Elementary School made public a commitment that was consolidated into one pledge and one goal. Today, our focus remains just as clear as it did when we first began.

Our Pledge

We are committed to creating a school that knows no limits to the academic success of each student.

Our One Goal

Every student, without exception and without excuse, will be proficient or advanced in reading, writing, and math.

Six Exceptional Systems

| Interventions |
| Data Management |
| Assessment Plan |
| Standards Alignment |
| Collaboration |
| Culture of Universal Achievement |

There is a difference between systems and "exceptional systems." Exceptional Systems are unique solutions to important challenges. They are created by the critical mass of a staff in a highly collaborative way. They are reviewed annually and driven by results. The six core exceptional systems that must be present on any successful campus should be visualized as a staircase. At the foundation is a **culture of universal achievement** that is grounded on the belief that every student is capable of meeting or exceeding grade level standards. When staff members believe that it is their responsibility to create success for every student, they **collaborate** as teams with that belief at their core. When they collaborate, they ensure that their work is **aligned to standards**. As they continue, they select common **assessments** that also align to those same standards. **Data** is then collected from common assessments in a way that is easily accessible, openly shared, and deliberately arranged. Finally, students are plugged into meaningful interventions that create academic results.

"We are committed to creating a school that knows no limits to the academic success of each student."

COLLABORATION COMMITMENT

As staff members of Los Pen, we are committed to collaborating with one another in a variety of ways. We understand that the greatest academic and social gains for our students come as a result of quality instruction from the classroom teacher and highly effective measures of collaboration among team members. Los Pen staff members work interdependently with their teams in many ways. The following are examples of individual commitments that we are all willing to make as we collaborate as a staff:

Clarity of Purpose: Team members remain driven by our one goal to ensure that each student is proficient or advanced in reading, writing, and math. They meet with a purpose and devise agendas and timelines to ensure success at every collaborative meeting. They take the time to decide upon meeting topics in advance. After meeting, they follow through with collective agreements as a team.

Respectful of Time: Los Pen staff members are action-oriented professionals who value one another's time. They are prompt to staff and team meetings. They make the most of their time by collaborating during the school day with colleagues as they creatively group students in an effort to meet every student's needs.

Wednesday Time-Banking: Every Wednesday afternoon from 2:15–3:40, we set aside time for teams to work closely as they design instruction that translates into academic achievement for all. This time is held sacred by all members of the team, and should not be used for personal appointments or individual work time. This time may be used for staff meetings once every other month.

Professional Growth: Los Pen staff members are open to learning new methods, ideas, and strategies that will lead to greater academic success for all. They participate in on-site Thursday Collaboration workshops. They seek ways to learn from one another, and are committed to growing professionally together.

Building Candid Professional Relationships: Los Pen staff members are committed to developing strong professional relationships with each other. They praise one another during times of individual, team, and school-wide success. They are honest with one another as they respectfully confront concerns through "Candid Collaboration." They support one another during times that are challenging both professionally and personally. They celebrate with one another as friends and colleagues outside of the school community.

Damen Lopez, Copyright 2009

244

"We are committed to creating a school that knows no limits to the academic success of each student."

STANDARDS ALIGNMENT

Our staff believes that we must continuously align our teaching to state standards. Standards alignment is not something that we've **done**, it's something that we do. In an effort to align our work in a practical way, we are committed to going through the process of dissecting each substandard. As we do, we ask ourselves four questions:

Specific Skills: What are the major skills that need to be targeted in order to effectively teach each sub-standard?

Assessments: What assessments will we use in order to offer summative and formative data for each sub-standard?

Instructional Methods: What strategies and ideas can we use to teach each sub-standard to our students?

Resources: What resources and materials will we use to ensure learning for all students? As we go forward, we understand that there are no shortcuts in doing this work. The best results will be realized when our teams work collaboratively together.

Damen Lopez, Copyright 2009

"We are committed to creating a school that knows no limits to the academic success of each student."

ASSESSMENT AND DATA ANALYSIS

This assessment plan was generated by the Los Peñasquitos Elementary School Staff. It expresses a collective commitment to participate in specific assessments throughout each school year. The process of generating this plan started with individual commitments by teachers to specific assessments within the classroom. Grade levels later came together to endorse a plan that would address the detailed assessment needs that they have as a team. Finally the Curriculum and Assessment committee, composed of teachers, classified staff, and support team members, took a detailed approach to ensure that we as a school participate in assessments that:

- ◆ Support the One Pledge and Goal of Our School
- ◆ Correlate to Academic Success for All
- ◆ Align with State Standards
- ◆ Encourage Student Participation Through the Development of Class and Individual Goals
- ◆ Focus on Assessments "FOR" Learning
- ◆ Facilitate Differentiated Instruction

We believe that careful follow-through on the assessments and goals within this plan will result in higher achievement for all students. All student data will be stored in a site database that is easily accessible. Data will be openly shared through articulation meetings three times a year. The insightful interpretation of specific student data will allow teachers to tailor their instruction to the unique needs of each student. This document is more than words on paper; it represents the hard work and commitment of this staff as we continue to strive for academic excellence.

WHAT CHARACTER MEANS FOR STUDENTS

TRUSTWORTHINESS

Be honest ◆ Don't deceive, cheat or steal ◆ Be reliable — do what you say you'll do ◆ Have the courage to do the right thing ◆ Build a good reputation ◆ Be loyal — stand by your family, friends and country

RESPECTFUL

Treat others with respect; follow the Golden Rule ◆ Be tolerant of differences ◆ Use good manners, not bad language ◆ Be considerate of the feelings of others ◆ Don't threaten, hit or hurt anyone ◆ Deal peacefully with anger, insults and disagreements

RESPONSIBLE

Do what you are supposed to do ◆ Persevere: keep on trying! ◆ Always do your best ◆ Use self-control ◆ Be self-disciplined ◆ Think before you act — consider the consequences ◆ Be accountable for your choices

FAIRNESS

Play by the rules • Take turns and share ◆ Be open-minded; listen to others ◆ Don't take advantage of others ◆ Don't blame others carelessly

CARING

Be kind ◆ Be compassionate and show you care ◆ Express gratitude ◆ Forgive others ◆ Help people in need

CITIZENSHIP

Do your share to make your school and community better ◆ Cooperate ◆ Get involved in community affairs ◆ Stay informed; vote ◆ Be a good neighbor ◆ Obey laws and rules ◆ Respect authority ◆ Protect the environment

CLASSROOM MANAGEMENT PLAN
(GRADES 2-5)

*"Character is doing the right thing,
even when no one is watching"*

CODE OF CONDUCT:

I will be trustworthy.   I will be respectful.   I will be fair.

I will be responsible.   I will be a good citizen.   I will be caring.

If you choose to break the code of conduct (consequences):

1ST TIME: **CAUTION: YELLOW**
Sign in the book.

2ND TIME: **STOP: RED**
Sign in the book. Fill out the rethinking paper

3RD TIME: **TIME-OUT:**
Sign in the Book
Take a Break in another class
Fill out the time-out letter/home to parent
Possible Loss of Recess

4TH TIME OR SEVERE DISRUPTION:
Immediately sent to the office
Fill out character violation

POSITIVE REINFORCEMENT:
Praise - Daily
Positive Notes Home — Random
Character Counts Award
Individual Classroom Reinforcement

We have read and discussed this classroom management plan and
will support and honor the plan throughout the year.

_____   _____

Parent Signature   Student Signature

 # RETHINKING LETTER

You are receiving a second warning about your negative choices. Please think about what you have done and answer these questions.

1. What did I do to receive my yellow warning?

_____

_____

2. What did I do to receive my red warning?

_____

_____

3. How did your choice affect others?

_____

_____

4. What caused your negative choice?

_____

_____

5. What could you do better next time?

_____

_____

Please check one:

_____ I get the point. I will try harder in class.

_____ I don't understand. We need to talk about my behavior.

_____   _____
Parent Signature   Student Signature

249

STAFF
CODE OF CONDUCT

The Los Pen staff is committed to modeling character to students, parents, and each other. Based on work that was conducted by our staff during the 2004-2005 school year, we commit to focusing on the six character pillars in the following ways:

TRUSTWORTHINESS

◆ Return borrowed items in a timely fashion
◆ File own books in Book Room
◆ No using copy codes accidentally left on machine
◆ Promptness to all meetings and duties

RESPECT

◆ Resolve conflicts peacefully
◆ Every idea is important
◆ Showing Active Listening
◆ Please and Thank You!
◆ Embrace differences
◆ Consider each other's feelings
◆ Tolerance
◆ Less of: Put downs. Don't lose faith or temperament.

BE ON TIME

◆ Be on time
◆ Be organized
◆ Ownership of actions and consequences
◆ Accountable for learning
◆ Less of: Blame of others.
◆ No Excuses

continued

STAFF
CODE OF CONDUCT *continued*

FAIRNESS

◆ Confidential with all
◆ Spotlighting fairness in our own lives
◆ Sharing work load among team/staff members
◆ Give people the benefit of the doubt

CARING

◆ Greet fellow staff members
◆ Stop and have genuine conversations
◆ Mention and discuss caring interactions with other teachers to students
◆ Sign cards for staff members
◆ Greet parents
◆ Give compliments
◆ Less of: Rumors and gossiping

CITIZENSHIP

◆ Vote
◆ Take care of our classrooms
◆ Respect for our school community
◆ Reach out to our community partners
◆ Teach citizenship to students
◆ Involvement at Canyon Rim Community Center
◆ Less of: Complaining about evening school-sponsored events.

NO EXCUSES

Damen Lopez, Copyright 2009

"We are committed to creating a school that knows no limits to the academic success of each student."

INTERVENTIONS

Good schools are able to take interventions and analyze their effectiveness through the use of data. Great schools, however, are able to take data and translate it directly into the creation of appropriate interventions. Our school is committed to providing interventions that generate academic and social success for all students.

ACADEMIC SYSTEM

Intense, Individual Interventions

Increased group time and smaller teacher/student ratios
- ◆ Fluency
- ◆ Comprehension
- ◆ Phonics

Targeted Group Interventions

Small Groups
- ◆ Fluency
- ◆ Comprehension
- ◆ Phonics

Increased Instructional time

Universal Interventions

Core Curriculum
Differentiation of Instruction
Master Schedule
Assessments
Articulation
Class Placement

BEHAVIORAL SYSTEM

Intense, Individual Interventions

Behavior Intervention Plan
Possible Referral to IAT

Targeted Group Interventions

Social Stories
Referral to Counseling/
Caring Connections
Behavior Support Plan
Referral to SST

Universal Interventions

Code of Conduct/School Rules
Universal Classroom
Management Plan
Morning Meetings
Resource Manual
Reinforcement System
Visual Schedule
Whole Class Social Skills
Behavior Contracts
Staff Development
Admin Connections/
Check-ins
Student Services
Recess Alternative
Class Placement

1-5% 1-5%

5-10% 5-10%

80-90% 80-90%

MY GOALS

_____

Student (Name)

_____

School Year

Subject: _____

My Goal for the trimester is: _____

_____

Three things that I can do to help me achieve my goal are:

1. _____

2. _____

3. _____

_____

Parent Signature

_____

Student Signature

_____

Teacher Signature

253

CALIFORNIA STATE FOURTH GRADE READING STANDARDS

1.0 WORD ANALYSIS, FLUENCY, AND SYSTEMATIC DEVELOPMENT

Students understand the basic features of reading. They select letter patterns and know how to translate them into spoken language by using phonics, syllabication, and word parts. They apply this knowledge to achieve fluent oral and silent reading.

COMPONENTS OF THE STANDARDS	SPECIFIC SKILLS	ASSESSMENTS	INSTRUCTIONAL METHODS	RESOURCES
WORD RECOGNITION				
1.1 Read narrative and expository text aloud with grade-appropriate fluency and accuracy and with appropriate pacing, intonation, and expression.	◆ Pacing ◆ Accuracy ◆ Intonation ◆ Expression	◆ IRI's ◆ DIBELS ◆ Fluency Timings ◆ Fluency Rubric	◆ Informal observations ◆ Anecdotal notes during guided reading ◆ Conferences ◆ Lit Circles ◆ Poem of the week ◆ Books on Tape ◆ Oral Presentation	◆ DIBELS ◆ Words Their Way ◆ 6-Min. Solutions ◆ Phonics They Use ◆ Rewards
VOCABULARY AND CONCEPT DEVELOPMENT				
1.2 Apply knowledge of word origins, derivations, synonyms, antonyms, and idioms to determine the meaning of words and phrases.	◆ Base Words (s,es,ed,ing,er,est) ◆ Idioms ◆ Synonyms ◆ Antonyms	◆ Theme Skills Test-HM (pages 14,15,44,60) ◆ HM Practice Sheets ◆ CA Summative Test (pages 4,25,47) ◆ Conferences ◆ Guided Reading ◆ Observation	◆ Guided reading ◆ Think aloud ◆ Idiom a day, discuss, post on chart ◆ Kids raise hand ◆ Games ◆ Use idioms in writing	◆ The King that Reigned ◆ Boss of the Plains-HM ◆ Internet - Google ◆ Book of Lists ◆ Frindle ◆ Wordly Wise Lesson

Standard	Concepts/Skills	Assessment	Activities	Resources
1.3 Use knowledge of root words to determine the meaning of unknown words within a passage.	• Roots (tele, rupt, sign, spect, graph, tract) • Compound Words	• Theme Skills Test — HM (Pages 39,58,127) • Use in Writing • HM Practice Pages	• Root word trees (involve parents) • Word Splash (Kids make dictionaries in journals) • Games memory • Teach physical signals • Compound Word Pics	• Words Their Way • Writer's Express • HM • puzzlemaker.com
1.4 Know common roots and affixes derived from Greek and Latin and use this knowledge to analyze the meaning of complex words (e.g., international).	• Roots- See Above • Prefixes (re, mis, pre, con, com, dis, un, inter) • Suffixes (ment, less, ly, y, er, or, ist, able, ible, ion, ness, ful)	• Theme Skills Test — HM (Pages 40, 59, 82, 84, 104,126,) • Spelling Tests • Guided Reading • Meaning of Prefixes and Suffixes	• Spelling Book • Word Sorts • Prefix/Suffix Trees • Word Hunt | Prefix	Root	Suffix
---	---	---		• Red Hot Root Words • Words Their Way • Scholastic-Prefix/Suffix Cards • Rewards

1.5 Use a thesaurus to determine related words and concepts.	• Teach all about how to use a thesaurus		• Use Thesaurus
			• HM-Overheads
			• Make overhead of words
			  — ask questions
			  — mini lesson	

1.6 Distinguish and interpret words with multiple meanings.				

LOS PENASQUITOS ELEMENTARY ASSESSMENT GRID

	SEPTEMBER	FEBRUARY	MAY
KINDERGARTEN	• Letter I.D. • Phonics Skills • Running Record • Math Skills Checklist	• Letter I.D. • Phonics Skills • Word Recognition • Phonemic Awareness • Sentence Dictation • Running Record • Math Skills Checklist • On Demand Writing	• Letter I.D. • Phonics Skills • Word Recognition • Phonemic Awareness • Sentence Dictation • Running Record • Math Skills 1 Prob. Solving • On Demand Writing
FIRST	• On Demand Writing • Spelling Inventory • Running Record / IRI • Math Skills Assessment 1 • Math Problem Solving	• On Demand Writing • Spelling Inventory • Running Record / IRI • Math Skills Assessment 2 • Math Problem Solving	• On Demand Writing • Spelling Inventory • Running Record / IRI • Math Skills Assessment 3 • Math Problem Solving
SECOND	• On Demand Writing • Running Record / IRI • Everyday Math Beg. Assessment • Math Problem Solving • Spelling Inventory • Fluency • MAPS (Read, Writ., Math)	• On Demand Writing • IRI • Everyday Math Mid-year • Math Problem Solving • Spelling Inventory • Fluency • MAPS (Read, Writ., Math)	• On Demand Writing • IRI • Everyday Math End of Year Assessment • Math Problem Solving • Spelling Inventory • Fluency • MAPS (Read, Writ., Math)

256

	Beginning	Mid-year	End of Year
THIRD	• On Demand Writing • Spelling Inventory • Spelling (No Excuses Words) • Everyday Math Beg. Assessment • On-Demand Prob. Solving • MAPS (Read, Writ., Math) • Fluency	• On Demand Writing • Spelling Inventory • Everyday Math Mid-year • MAPS (Read, Writ., Math) • Fluency	• On Demand Writing • Spelling Inventory • Everyday Math End of Year Assessment • On-Demand Math Prob. Solving • MAPS (Read, Writ., Math) • Fluency
FOURTH	• On Demand Writing (Response to Lit) • GATES – Form S (Acad. October) • Everyday Math Beg. Assessment • Spelling – Word Journeys • MAPS (Read, Writ., Math) • Fluency (students under 150 wpm)	• On Demand Writing • Everyday Math Mid-year • Spelling – Word Journeys • MAPS (Read, Writ., Math) • Fluency	• On Demand Writing • Everyday Math End of Year Assessment • Spelling – Word Journeys • Fluency • MAPS (Read, Writ., Math)
FIFTH	• On Demand Writing (Persuasive Essay) • GATES – Form S (Acad. October) • Everyday Math Beg. Assessment • Spelling – Word Journeys • MAPS (Read, Writ., Math) • Fluency (students under 150 wpm)	• On Demand Writing • Everyday Math Mid-year • Spelling – Word Journeys • MAPS (Read, Writ., Math) • Fluency	• On Demand Writing • Everyday Math End of Year Assessment • Spelling – Word Journeys • Fluency • MAPS (Read, Writ., Math)

257

Student Involvement in Assessment

The staff at Los Peñasquitos Elementary believes that one of the best ways to increase student achievement is to involve students in the assessment process. Below is an example of the ways that third grade teachers will involve students in the process. Each grade level has made a similar commitment based on the assessments used by their team.

3rd Grade's Commitment to Involving Students in the Assessment Process	
On Demand Writing	Teachers will share the "six traits" child friendly rubrics with their students. We will involve the students in the scoring process, starting with the whole class and working towards individual peer scoring. Teachers will continue to guide students toward mastery in the first three traits, "ideas, organization, and conventions". Teachers will add "word choice", as a new area of focus.
Problem Solving	Teachers will also share "Problem Solving" child friendly rubrics with their students and involve them in the scoring process. Students will practice scoring with their peers.

SPELLING INVENTORY	Teachers will share scores with their students. We will explain the spelling stages and make the students aware of their current stage. Teachers will help students set individual goals for themselves based on their needs and group accordingly.
MATH SKILL ASSESSMENT	Teachers will meet with students individually to discuss results of the Math Basic Skills Test. All students will receive a check-off sheet highlighting the test items that they have not yet mastered. Teachers will assist students in setting goals for the future.
FLUENCY	Teachers will receive training from Gail Adams in " Fluency Timings". Students will participate in fluency timings at least three times a week. Students will score themselves and chart growth. Teachers will instruct students on how to make individual goals for themselves.
IRI	Teachers will share IRI results including miscues, retelling, and comprehension. We will communicate students' strengths and weaknesses and help students create goals for the future.
MAPS	Teachers will share scores with their students and will set goals with them. Teachers will share Lexile ranges with students to use at home. We will work towards involving parents as we gain experience with MAPS.

APPENDIX B

NO EXCUSES
UNIVERSITY

No Excuses
University
Three-Way Pledge

Teacher Pledge

I am committed to creating a school that knows no limits to the academic success of each student. The following represents my personal commitment to the academic success of every student at Los Peñasquitos Elementary School:

- ◆ Accept no limits on the learning potential of any child
- ◆ Meet the individual learning needs of each child
- ◆ Create serious classroom learning environments
- ◆ Treat students, parents, and colleagues with courtesy and respect
- ◆ Hold students, parents, and each other to the highest standards of performance.
- ◆ Collaborate regularly with colleagues to seek and implement more effective strategies for helping each child to achieve his or her academic potential
- ◆ Do whatever it takes - go the extra mile - to ensure that every student achieves or exceeds grade level expectations based on state academic standards

_____   _____

Teacher Signature   Date

Teacher + Student + Parent = Success

Damen Lopez, Copyright 2009

262

No Excuses University Three-Way Pledge

continued

Student Pledge

I understand that my education is very important to my future. It will help me develop the tools I need to become a successful and productive person. I know that my education now will prepare me for college in the future. Because of this I am committed to following the requirements found in my No Excuses University Student Handbook. In addition, I commit to:

- Arriving at school everyday on time unless I am ill
- Following the rules and the six pillars of character of our school
- Completing and turning in homework on time every day
- Returning letters, corrected work, and other school materials to my parents

---

Student Signature   Date

Teacher + Student + Parent = Success

No Excuses University Three-Way Pledge

continued

Parent Pledge

I understand that my child's education today is essential for their success in life. This experience will support him/her to become a successful and productive person. It will also prepare them for college if they so choose to attend. Because of this I am committed to following the requirements found in my No Excuses University Parent Handbook. These responsibilities are found in the:

♦ Mission, Vision, Shared Commitment, and Goal of Los Peñasquitos

♦ Parent Code of Conduct

♦ "Take Five" Commitment

♦ Parent Goals Commitment

♦ Commitment to ensuring my child attends school on time every day unless they are ill

Each of these responsibilities speaks to my commitment to support Los Peñasquitos in order to ensure a bright future for my child.

_____   _____

Parent Signature   Date

TEACHER + STUDENT + PARENT = SUCCESS

Damen Lopez, Copyright 2009

"We are committed to creating a school that knows no limits to the academic success of each student."

No Excuses University Pledge

COLLEGE VOCABULARY BY GRADE LEVEL

Below are the words that each grade level has committed to using in their classes as we promote college readiness for all. Please work with your team to continuously expose students to the college vocabulary within your grade's column, as well as all the grades before you.

GRADE:	VOCABULARY WORDS	
K	College	
1st	Achieve Graduate	Career Goal
2nd	Major Professor Dormitory	Mascot Scholarship
3rd	Advisor Application Dean's List GPA Loan Research	Alumni Bachelor's Degree Finals Grants NCAA
4th/5th	All words K-3 Focus on A-G	

Damen Lopez, Copyright 2009

> *"We are committed to creating a school that knows no limits to the academic success of each student."*
>
> No Excuses University Pledge

2006-2007
COLLEGE READINESS

GRADES: K-3

The planning committee came to the understanding that instead of strictly promoting the A-G requirements, we will focus on promoting awareness about college. We believe that this can and should look differently across the grade levels. See below for the ways that each grade will be asked to promote this awareness.

◆ Utilize college vocabulary in each classroom

◆ Participate in a college readiness kick-off assembly

◆ Promote college readiness at Friday Flags

◆ Add questions to the yearly school climate survey

◆ Continue to promote the idea of college in creative ways deemed appropriate by each grade level

◆ Change Olympic Field Day to College Field Day
◆ All classes have a chant for their university
◆ All classes participate in individual student goals conferences where they explain data and assessment to students.

continued

2006-2007
COLLEGE READINESS *continued*

GRADES: 4-5

◆ Participate in a college readiness kick-off assembly

◆ Discuss the importance of students being on the A-G track in high school

◆ Display A-G requirement posters

◆ Talk about different college options

◆ Help students understand that if they want to work in a specific profession that there are decisions that they can begin to make now as they choose their track to college

◆ Decide upon specific strategies that will be promoted at each grade level to support college readiness (Cornell notes, use of planners, etc.)

◆ Support the idea of students being accountable for their learning

◆ Introduce authentic college readiness tools that students will see in high school (Enrollment packets, etc.)

◆ Continue to take field trips to college campuses

◆ Encourage parents and students to attend the yearly college fair at the convention center

◆ Change Olympic Field Day to College Field Day

◆ All classes have a chant for their university

◆ All classes participate in individual student goals conferences where they explain data and assessment to students.

NEU PARENTING GOALS

Every family plays a key role in supporting the academic and social growth of a No Excuses University Student. Just as students set academic goals, parents should also set goals to support the success of their child. Below is a template used for parents to develop two very important goals. First, parents should develop one goal to support the academics of their child. Second, plans should be made to continue to support the social and emotional growth of their student through a goal to enhance parenting skills. Both goals should include specific steps that will be taken to ensure success.

ACADEMIC GOAL	GOAL TO ENHANCE PARENTING
GOAL:	**GOAL:**
_____	_____
_____	_____
STEPS FOR SUCCESS:	**STEPS FOR SUCCESS:**
_____	_____
_____	_____
_____	_____

No Excuses University
at Los Peñasquitos
Student Handbook

This book belongs to:

_____

The year I graduate college:

_____

Dear Students,

Welcome to the No Excuses University at Los Peñasquitos. This year you will learn like never before as we prepare your path to college. Each and every one of you has very special academic and social gifts. These gifts are seen on a daily basis in the way that you work hard in the classroom in reading, writing, and math. They are also seen in the way that you display character by focusing on the six character traits described in this handbook. As you read through this handbook, you will learn about the expectations we have for all students of the No Excuses University at Los Peñasquitos. I promise that you will be successful if you remember these two words, **No Excuses**. "No Excuses" is not just our motto, it is our commitment as students, parents, and staff to do whatever it takes to be successful in school. I know that you are capable of being a great student. I am proud of you and I look forward to celebrating your successes throughout the 2005 – 2006 school year!

Sincerely,

Mr. Lopez
Principal

# No Excuses University
at Los Peñasquitos
Student Handbook

No Excuses Student Handbook
Table of Contents

A complete copy of our Los Peñasquitos
No Excuses University Student Handbook
is available for download at
www.turnaroundschools.com

GETTING STARTED:
JOINING THE
NEU NETWORK

Dear Principal,

Thank you for your interest in the No Excuses University. Since the creation of the NEU Network in the spring of 2006, we have had the tremendous opportunity to help change the lives of thousands of students across this nation. It is our hope that your application to join our network will be a successful one and thus continue to add to this revolution.

As you know, we do not charge for this application, nor do we ask for any annual dues to be a part of the NEU Network ...

APPLICATION CHECKLIST

Before you mail your application, please review and understand the following items listed below. (Additional information is available at www.turnaroundschools.com.)

☑ Has a team of staff members, including your principal, attended a TurnAround Schools Institute?

☑ Please note that all applications will be reviewed by the NEU Selection Committee within 30 days of their receipt. Those listed as the "contact" will be informed of a decision within this time period.

☑ Remember, while every application will be thoroughly reviewed, not every school will be invited to join the NEU Network of Schools.

☑ Please note that schools invited into the NEU Network will be required to take part in a yearly re-application review. While this process is far less intensive than this original application, it is intended to ensure the continued successful implementation of the NEU model. Only schools who display consistent success and improvement will be asked to remain within the NEU Network of Schools.

☑ Has your staff adopted individual universities for each classroom?

☑ Did you include your application cover sheet?

☑ Did you include your written application containing documentation about the six exceptional systems and powerful symbolism?

☑ Did you include your DVD/Video?

A complete copy of the
No Excuses University Application Packet
is available at
www.TurnAroundSchools.com

Course Catalog
2008-2009

Vermont Elementary School
3695 Vermont Street
San Bernadino, CA 92407
(909)880-6658

A complete copy of the
Vermont Parent University Course Catalog
is available at
www.TurnAroundSchools.com

BIBLIOGRAPHY

Alliance for Excellent Education. (2006). *Saving futures, saving dollars: The impact of education on crime reduction and earnings.* Washington, D.C.: Alliance for Excellent Education.

Baum, S., & Ma, J. (2007, January). *Education pays 2007: The benefits of higher education for individuals and society.* Retrieved August 11, 2009 from College Board Web site: http://www.collegeboard.com/prod_downloads/about/news_info/cbsenior/yr2007/ed-pays-2007.pdf

Bureau of Labor Statistics. (2006). Average number of jobs started by individuals from age 18 to age 42 in 1978-2006 by age and sex. *National Longitudinal Surveys.* Retrieved August 11, 2009 from http://www.bls.gov/nls/y79r22jobsbyage.pdf.

275

Bureau of Labor Statistics. (2007). *College enrollment and work activity of high school graduates.* [Press release] Retrieved August 11, 2009 from http://www.bls.gov/ news.release/archives/hsgec_04252008.htm

Bureau of Labor Statistics. (2008). *Volunteering in the United States.* Washington, D.C.: The U.S. Department of Labor, Bureau of Labor Statistics.

Bureau of Labor Statistics. (2009a). *Education pays.* Retrieved August 11, 2009 from http://www.bls.gov/emp/emptab7. htm

Bureau of Labor Statistics. (2009b). *Labor Force Statistics from the Current Population Survey.* Retrieved August 11, 2009 from http://www.bls.gov/cps/

Conley, D.T. (2005). *College knowledge: What it really takes for students to succeed and what we can do to get them ready.* Hoboken, N.J.: Jossey-Bass.

Day, J.C., & Newburger, E.C. (2002, July). *The big payoff: educational attainment and synthetic estimates of work-life earnings.* U.S. Census Bureau. Washington, D.C.: U.S. Government Printing Office.

Federal Trade Commission. (2008, July 29). *FTC report sheds new light on food marketing to children and adolescents.* [Press release]. Retrieved August 11, 2009 from http:// www.ftc.gov/opa/2008/07/foodmkting.shtm

Harlem Children's Zone. (2009). *Harlem children's zone.*

Retrieved August 11, 2009 from http://www.hcz.org/

Henderson, P. (2009, February 10). U.S. judges seek massive California prisoner release. *Reuters*. Retrieved August 11, 2009 from http://www.reuters.com/article/topNews/idUSTRE5190CB20090210

Johnson, M.C. (2008, December 10). Prepping for college — in elementary school. *The Press-Enterprise*. Retrieved August 11, 2009 from http://www.pe.com/localnews/inland/stories/PE_News_Local_S_nexcuses11.4702b37.html

Josephson Institute. (2009). *Character education program: Character counts*. Retrieved August 11, 2009 from http://charactercounts.org/

Kinsey, T., Jemal, A., Liff, J., Ward, E., & Thun, M. Secular trends in mortality from common cancers in the United States by educational attainment, 1993–2001. *Journal of the National Cancer Institute*, 100, 1003–12.

Lopez, D. (2009, January/February). College readiness for all: What's the alternative? NAESP's *Principal Magazine*, 50-51.

Marketing Charts. (2008, January 23). *Super Bowl ad spend totaled $1.84B over 20 years, rates quadrupled*. Retrieved August 11, 2009 from http://www.marketingcharts.com/television/super-bowl-ad-spend-totaled-184b-over-20-years-rates-quadrupled-3153/

Marklein, M.B. (2008, August 1). U.S. community colleges at a 'turning point.' *USA Today.* Retrieved August 11, 2009 from http://www.usatoday.com/news/education/2008-07-22-comcol-main_N.htm

Meara, E.R., Richards, S., & Cutler, D.M. (2008). The gap gets bigger: Changes in mortality and life expectancy, by education, 1981–2000. *Health Affairs,* 27(2), 350–60.

Ransdell, E. (1999, December). The Nike story? Just tell it!. *Fast Company Magazine,* 31. Retrieved August 11, 2009 from http://www.fastcompany.com/magazine/31/nike.html

Reinberg, S. (2008, July 8). College-educated fare better when cancer strikes. *U.S. News and World Report.* Retrieved August 11, 2009 from http://health.usnews. com/articles/health/healthday/2008/07/08/college-educated-fare-better-when-cancer-strikes.html

Riemer, J. (2001, February 10). Perlman makes his music — the hard way. *The Houston Chronicle,* E8.

Riordan, J. (2008, February 28). *Pew report finds more than one in 100 adults are behind bars.* [Press release]. Retrieved August 11, 2009 from the Pew Center on the States Web site: http://www.pewcenteronthestates.org/news_room_detail.aspx?id=35912

Rupert, P, & Stepanczuk, C. (2007, March). Women in the workforce. *April 2007 Economic Trends.* Retrieved August 11, 2009 from Federal Reserve Bank of Cleveland Web site: http://www.clevelandfed.org/research/trends/2007/ 0407/03ecoact.cfm

Safer, Morley. (Correspondent). (2002). The mensch of Malden Mills. [Television series episode]. In D. Hewitt (Producer), *60 minutes*. New York: CBS.

Smalley, L. (Director). (2008). Darius goes west. [Motion picture]. United States: Roll With Me Productions.

U.S. Department of Agriculture. (2009). *Supplemental nutritional assistance program.* Retrieved August 11, 2009 from http://www.fns.usda.gov/snap/

U.S. Department of Health and Human Services. (2009). *The 2009 HHS poverty guidelines.* Retrieved August 11, 2009 from http://aspe.hhs.gov/poverty/09poverty.shtml

Vock, D. C. (2006, August 3). Medicaid: Biggest insurer is a budget buster. *Stateline.org.* Retrieved August 11, 2009 from http://www.stateline.org/live/ViewPage.action?site NodeId=136&languageId=1&contentId=131622

A sincere and special thanks to my design and editing team for all their hard work — for offering candor that did not break my confidence and suggestions that did not ruin the substance of this book. It has been my pleasure to work so closely with each of you.

Shendl Diamond
LikeMindsPress.com

Kaitlin Barr
Editor
kaitlin.n.barr@gmail.com

Catherine Perry
Cover Design
CPerryDesigns.com

Katie MacLeod
Cover Portrait Photo
CandidsByKatie.com

Fran Hjalmarson
Supporting Editor
fran@turnaroundschools.com

Kim Melvin
Supporting Editor

Carolyn Ottoson
Supporting Editor